# TWIST • WRAP • WEAVE

# Colorful
# Wirework Jewelry

**Kalmbach Books**
21027 Crossroads Circle
Waukesha, Wisconsin 53186
www.JewelryAndBeadingStore.com

Published in 2016
20 19 18 17 16    1 2 3 4 5

Manufactured in China.

**ISBN:** 978-1-62700-316-2
**EISBN:** 978-1-62700-317-9

**Editor:** Dianne Wheeler
**Book Design:** Lisa Bergman
**Technical Editor:** Karin Van Voorhees
**Photographer:** William Zuback

**Library of Congress Control Number:** 2016931488

# TWIST • WRAP • WEAVE

# Colorful
## Wirework Jewelry

## Kim St. Jean

KALMBACH BOOKS

Waukesha, Wisconsin

# Contents

## WEAVING

# INTRODUCTION

**W**ire and I go way back. I started working in wire when I was seven years old. Yep, that's right, I was making and selling wire-wrapped rings when I was seven years old. I'm an Army brat, and being such, people moved in and out of their quarters almost on a daily basis. That being said, I had an endless supply of telephone cable wire. I'd hang around watching the phone man install the new lines and then swoop in during clean-up for all of the left-over wire scrap. The men were always obliging in letting me help clean up—hmmm...

That telephone wire soon became tiny baskets for Barbie and her friend's luxury house (modeled off the set of Dick Van Dyke–what a great house!) and rings for all of our neighbors who were fortunate enough to live in my sales territory—the cul-de-sac. These items accompanied my lines of macramé bracelets, fatigue boot blousers as anklets, matching ladybug paper weights and refrigerator magnets made from painted rocks, Barbie doll custom furniture made from thimbles and pizza box stabilizers, Mom's sewing remnant braided rugs and woven wall hangings hung with those awesome little hangers that socks came on, my very fragrant perfume, and something sort of edible made from Vienna sausages, water, and pickle juice. Door-to-door entrepreneurship—that's what it was!

But, when people ask, "How'd you get started in this business?" I usually offer an abbreviated version that starts a little later. In 1998, I finally got a business license and started my own business. I started selling vintage kimonos and other vintage Asian art.

This soon morphed into vintage clothing and jewelry. In January 2000, I opened a boutique selling a variety of items my mother and I made, including refurbished jewelry. By 2001, Norm joined me and we moved to a wholesale merchandise mart where we became a full-time beads and findings wholesale supplier to the trade.

I continued to design, mostly in beads, but soon moved on as many of us do. Moving from beads to wire is the natural progression most of us follow. I am best known for my metalwork, but I have a love of wire that still lingers. My love of color stems from my beading days and time as a Swarovski Ambassador.

I am forever evolving; I make it my habit to learn a new skill every year, sometimes in jewelry, sometimes not. But I never completely close any door from my past endeavors–barring Vienna sausage, of course.

When I re-visited wireworking, I was drawn to the newly-available colored wire. I began aggressively designing bright, colorful pieces to utilize the wire to its best potential.

I hope you enjoy the ideas I'm sharing!

## About the projects

The projects in this book are for all levels. Whether you have never worked with wire or if you have done wirework for years, you will enjoy these projects. I have limited the tools to those easily found at your local bead shop or large hobby store and have made suggestions for alternative tools if I use specialty ones.

In almost all of the projects, I have used fellow artists' work for my focal pieces. However, you can easily substitute with similar pieces if you don't have the exact components or colors I used—take the technique and run with it, be creative, substitute, or add. Let your style shine through.

# Basics

# TOOLS

## Basic Tool Kit

The tools in the Basic Tool Kit are the ones you will need for most every project in this book. You can start out with inexpensive tools purchased at your local hobby shop. The pliers should be "jewelry pliers," not the kind from a hardware store. You can purchase these pliers individually or packaged in a set.

**Chainnose pliers** have flat inner jaws and tappered tips for gripping wire. You will often use these pliers in tandem with other pliers to make loops or to open and close jump rings.

**Flatnose pliers** are similar to chainnose pliers, but have flat, outer jaws, making it easier to make sharper bends in the wire.

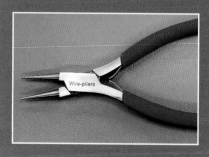

**Roundnose pliers** are critical for making loops and bends in wire. These pliers have tapered, conical jaws and are perfect for shaping wire.

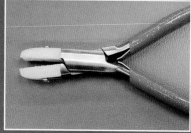

**Nylon-jaw pliers** feature a nylon lining in the jaws, which protects the wire from nicks and marks. They are used for straightening wire.

**Flush wire cutters** leave less of a slant when used to cut wire. One side of the cut will be flush, while the other side will be slightly beveled.

## Specialty tools

These are tools I may use in specific projects. These are not part of your Basic Tool Kit, but will come in handy for various techniques.

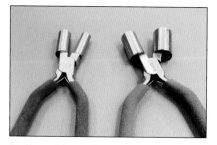

**Bail-making pliers** are pliers that have two dfferent sized jaws. They are used to form consistent bails, wrapped loops, and small jump rings.

**Bench blocks and anvils** provide a hard, smooth surface on which to use your chasing hammer when flattening wire.

A **domed chasing hammer** has a flat head on one side and a domed, round head on the other. Use this kind of hammer to strike against another tool to flatten a rounded-wire surface.

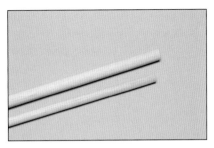

**Dowels** are circular rods frequently made from wood, used for shaping wire into coils and rings.

A **draw plate** is a metal or wooden plate with holes drilled through the surface in varying sizes. Wire can be pulled through the holes to make it a uniform size and shape.

A **hand punch** is used with a chasing hammer to make holes in a metal surface (like a flattened piece of wire).

**The Mister Twister coil maker** is a device with a rotating handle that attches to coil mandrels. Thread the wire through the device, rotate the crank holding the wire, and you can make consistently perfect coils. This is also an efficient and economic device for making your own jump rings.

A **ring clamp** will hold wire projects while you are working on them. The wedge insert accommodates coils of different sizes.

A **wire rounder** is a tool to de-burr the end of wire after it has been cut. This tool is perfect to smooth the ends of earrring wires.

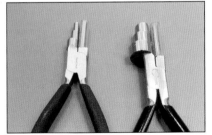

**Wrap 'n' Tap pliers** are stepped roundnose pliers used for bending wire into consistent sized loops. One side of the pliers has a flat, rubber surface and the other side has a series of three round surfaces that increase in diameter with each step.

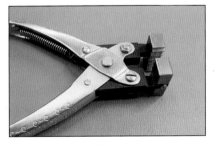

**Zig-Zag parallel bending pliers** reduce repetitive wrist motion and save time because you can create several zig-zags at once.

# TECHNIQUES

## Crochet

### Chain stitch

Make a loop in the thread, crossing the ball end over the tail. Put the hook through the loop, yarn over the hook, and draw through the first loop. Then, yarn over the hook and draw through the loop. Repeat for the desired number of chain stitches.

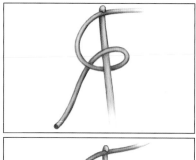

### Single crochet

Insert the hook through the front and back loops of the next stitch. Yarn over and draw through the stitch. Yarn over and draw through both remaining loops.

### Bead single crochet

Before starting a single crochet, slide a bead against the base of the loop on the hook. Work normally. The beads will be on the side facing away from you.

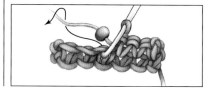

### Slip stitch

Go into the next stitch. Yarn over and draw the yarn through the stitch and the loop.

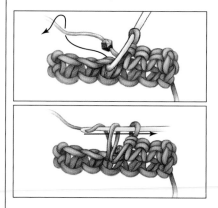

### Bead slip stitch

Go into the next stitch. Slide a bead down to the hook, yarn over, and bring the yarn through both the stitch and the loop on the hook.

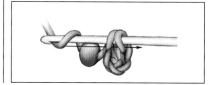

## Making a plain loop

**1** If making a plain loop above a bead, trim the wire ³⁄₈" above the bead. Using chainnose pliers, make a right-angle bend close to the bead. If working with a naked piece of wire, make a bend ¼" from the end **(a)**.
**2** Grasp the tip of the wire with roundnose pliers and roll the wire to form a half circle **(b)**.
**3** Reposition the pliers in the loop and continue rolling, forming a centered circle above the bead **(c)**.
**4** This is the finished loop **(d)**.

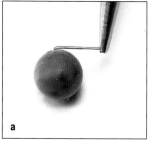

a

b

c

d

## Making a wrapped loop

**1** Using chainnose pliers, make a right-angle bend in the wire about 2 mm above a bead or other component or at least 1¼" from the end of a naked piece of wire **(a)**.

**2** Position the jaws of the roundnose pliers in the bend. The closer to the tip of the pliers that you work, the smaller the loop will be **(b)**.

**3** Curve the short end of the wire over the top jaw of the roundnose pliers **(c)**.

**4** Reposition the pliers so the lower jaw fits snugly in the loop. Curve the wire downward around the bottom jaw of the pliers. This is the first half of a wrapped loop **(d)**.

**5** To complete the wraps, grasp the top of the loop with one pair of pliers **(e)**.

**6** With another pair of pliers, wrap the wire around the stem two or three times. Trim the excess wire and gently press the cut end close to the wraps with chainnose pliers **(f)**.

## Wrapping leather cord ends

**1** Cut two 6" pieces of 18-gauge wire. Make a loop 1" from the end of the wire at about the ⅛" "mark" on your roundnose pliers. Stop the loop when the wire forms a "p" **(a)**.

**2** Place the end of the leather over the "p" so the length of the leather is running parallel to the long portion of the "p" **(b)**.

**3** Hold the leather on the circle of the "p" with chainnose pliers in your non-dominant hand **(c)**.

**4** Begin wrapping the long end of the wire around the leather, beginning against the side of the chainnose pliers. Do this as tight as you can and coil the loops against each other **(d)**.

**5** End the last loop, making sure it is not on the short leg of the "p." Using flush wire cutters, cut the wire at an angle **(e)**.

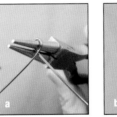
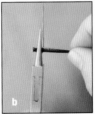
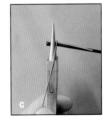
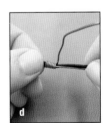

**6** Press the last wire into the leather with your chainnose pliers **(f)**.

**7** Fold back the loop of the "p" with chainnose pliers and cut away the leather.

**8** This is a completed leather cord with a wrapped end **(g)**.

## Making an S-hook clasp

**1** Cut a 2½" piece of 16-gauge wire. Using your chainnose pliers, make a very tight pinch at the end of the wire **(a)**.

**2** Repeat on the other end of the wire, but make the pinch coil in the opposite direction **(b)**.

**3** Your pinch looks like the head of a "swan". Place the chin of the swan on the rubber part of your Wrap 'n' Tap pliers, behind the middle barrel **(c)**.

**4** Pull the long end of the wire tightly up and over the barrel of the Wrap 'n' Tap pliers until the wire touches the back of your "swan's" head (or the pinched end) **(d)**.

**5** Slide the wire off of the pliers and repeat with the other end of the wire **(e)**. This time, the "chin" faces away.

**6** Using the chasing hammer and anvil, hammer the curve of the hook on both ends **(f)**.

**7** This is a picture of the finished "S" hook **(g)**.

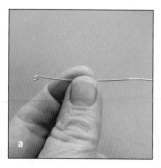
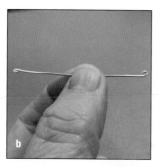
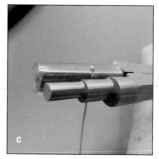
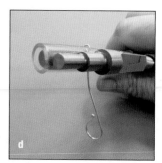

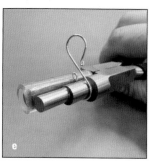

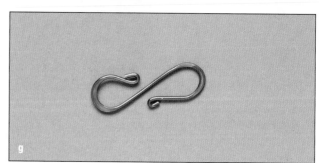

## Making jump rings

**1** Working off of the spool, position the end of your wire in the center of the Wrap 'n' Tap pliers, between the rubber and metal so the wire is not sticking out the opposite side of the pliers **(a)**.

**2** Twist your wrist away from your body while firmly holding the wire against the metal barrel.

**3** Open and shut the pliers as you twist the wire around the plier barrel.

**4** Continue wrapping until you have as many rings as you need.

**5** Use flush wire cutters to cut the rings **(b)**.

**6** This is a picture of completed jump rings **(c)**.

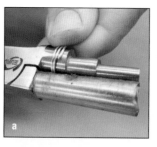
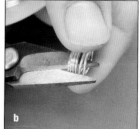

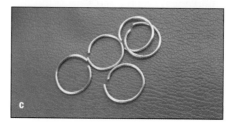

## Making a shepherd's hook clasp

**1** Cut a 2½" piece of 16-gauge wire. Using your chainnose piers, make a very tight pinch at the end of the wire **(a)**.

**2** The pinch looks like the head of a swan. Place the chin of the swan on the rubber part of your Wrap 'n' Tap pliers, behind the middle barrel **(b)**.

**3** Pull the long end of the wire tightly up and over the barrel of the Wrap 'n' Tap pliers until the wire touches the back of your "swan's" head (or the pinched end) **(c)**.

**4** Slide the wire off of the pliers and position chainnose or roundnose pliers on the wire tail even to the pinch of the loop.

**5** Bend the "neck" directly behind the loop to create a shepherd's hook **(d)**. Position your pliers about ⅛" above the loop of your hook and bend the tail down over the pliers at a 90-degree angle **(e)**.

**6** Pull the wire down so it is pointing directly at the table **(f)**.

**7** Bring the wire back up and under the pliers creating a loop.

**8** Wrap the wire to finish a wrapped loop (Techniques, p. 11) **(g)**.

**9** Cut away the excess wire **(h)**.

**10** Hammer the curve of the hook with your domed chasing hammer **(i)**.

**11** This is a completed shepherd's hook clasp **(j)**.

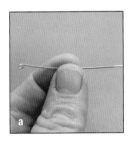  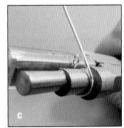  

 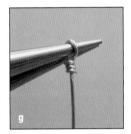 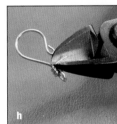  

## Opening and closing loops and jump rings

**1** Hold a loop or a jump ring with two pairs of pliers, such as chainnose, flatnose, or bentnose pliers **(a)**.

**2** To open the loop or jump ring, bring the tips of one pair of pliers toward you, and push the tips of the other pair away from you **(b)**.

**3** This is the open jump ring **(c)**. Reverse the steps to close.

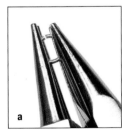 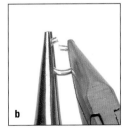 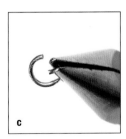

## Making a toggle ring and toggle bar

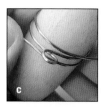

**Toggle ring**

**1** Select a dowel or other round object in the size you would like for the ring of your toggle.

**2** Cut an 18" piece of 18-gauge wire from your coil. Using roundnose pliers, make a loop in the center of the wire **(a)**.

**3** Position the wire loop on the dowel. Wrap each end of the wire around the dowel one time in opposite directions **(b)**.

**4** Wrap the ends of the wire around the dowel a second time, wrapping the wires on opposite sides of the loop **(c)**.

**5** Wrap both ends of the wire around the dowel a third time, making sure the wires are on opposite sides of the loop **(d)**.

**6** Bring both wires around to the front of the dowel, parallel with the loop. Slide the toggle ring off of the dowel **(e)**.

**7** Holding the ring in your non-dominant hand, loop one of the wires under and through the ring **(f)**.

**8** Coil the wire tail around the ring **(g)**.

**9** Trim the excess wire with wire cutters. Using your chainnose pliers, tuck in the wire **(h, i)**.

**10** Repeat steps 7–9 on the other side of the loop.

**11** Cut a 6" piece of 18-gauge wire and coil it around the center bottom of the ring. Remove the excess wire with your wire cutters. Using your chainnoise pliers, tuck in the end of the wire **(j)**.

**12** This is a completed toggle ring **(k)**.

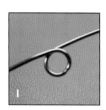

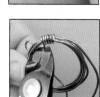
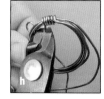
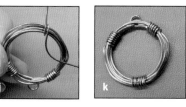

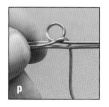

**Toggle bar**

**13** Cut a 12" piece of 18-gauge wire. Make a loop in the center of the wire with your roundnose pliers **(l)**.

**14** Position the wire loop inside the toggle ring with the loop up against one side. Grasp the wire with roundnose pliers against the outside of the toggle ring **(m)**.

**15** Bend the wire around the roundnose pliers and bring the wire back to the loop. Repeat on the other side of the toggle bar **(n)**.

**16** Pinch the ends together with nylon-jaw pliers **(o)**.

**17** Wrap one of the ends up and over the bar on the opposite side of the loop **(p)**.

**18** Coil the wire around the bar several times **(q)**.

**19** Repeat steps 18 and 19 on the opposite side of the loop **(r)**. Trim the wire ends.

**20** Use the toggle ring and bar together to make a special clasp **(s)**.

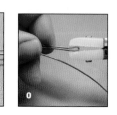

## Making earring wires

**1** Cut two 3" pieces of 20-gauge wire with flush wire cutters. Make a flush cut on each end **(a)**.

**2** String 1" of wire through the hole in the earring component and bend the wire straight up and parallel with the longer end of the wire.

**3** Position the roundnose pliers directly above the earring component to work as a space maker **(b)**.

**4** Pull the short end of the wire down across the long wire, parallel with the roundnose pliers **(c)**.

**5** Pinch the long wire so it is going straight up from the pliers. Wrap the short wire around the long wire in a very tight coil **(d)**.

**6** Place the long wire behind the large barrel of the Wrap 'n' Tap pliers, as far up as the coil will allow without being pinched **(e)**.

**7** Push the coil into the rubber of the pliers **(f)**.

**8** Pull the long end of the wire up and over the large barrel of the Wrap 'n' Tap pliers until the long wire touches the coil **(g)**.

**9** Hammer the curve of the wire on your anvil with a smooth domed hammer **(h)**.

**10** Repeat steps 3–8 for the second earring. Flush cut both earring wires to the same length **(i)**.

**11** This is a picture of a completed earring wire **(j)**.

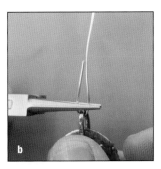
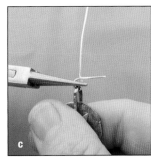
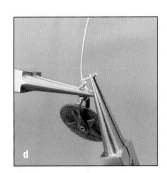

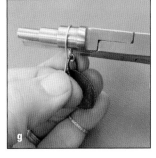
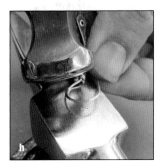

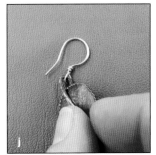

# About the WIRE

This book is about making jewelry using colored wire. Traditionally, raw nonferrous wire (meaning wire that contains no iron) is used for jewelry: gold, sterling silver, fine silver, copper, brass and bronze. Jewelry makers also use gold-filled, silver-filled, gold-plated, silver-plated, and Argentium. While these are the typical metals seen in everyday jewelry, now we have more options, including stainless steel, steel, aluminum, anodized aluminum, and *colored wire.*

Not all colored wires are the same. There are quite a few varieties to choose from. The colored wire I use in this book was produced by *Parawire.* There are other brands, and I suggest you try them to decide which you prefer.

I typically use sterling silver, copper, nickel, red brass, and yellow brass in my jewelry, so I had a learning curve in creating these projects. I discovered colored wire doesn't typically work-harden, which means in some cases it is difficult to make the wire maintain its shape, especially when working with the aluminum. I am accustomed to making a shape, hammering it, and it staying that way—but that didn't always work. So I designed projects that didn't require work-hardening.

I discovered if I used a very smooth hammer, I could hammer to a certain degree to achieve a shape that I wanted. Some of the colors heldup better than others when hammered, but in a few cases, there was some loss of color. You will have to decide if this is acceptable for your project or not. I decided I could forgo a little color for a shape or technique.

I learned not all colored wire is copper with a color coating. Some of the copper wire is silver-plated and then colored to facilitate the absolute best colors possible. There are some colored wires that are actually enamel over copper wire. The enameled wire is a stronger coloring technique.

Aluminum wire is soft, but very easy to shape. It's great for tighter techniques, but not so good for large forms like neck wires. Unfortunately, it will not work-harden.

Jewelry wire and other nonferrous metal wire is measured in gauges or millimeters. The American Wire Gauge (AWG), also known as Brown and Sharpe (B&S), is the system used almost universally in the United States and Canada. All gauges in this book refer to AWG standard.

When choosing wire, the smaller the gauge number, the thicker the wire. For example, 10-gauge wire is thicker than 20-gauge wire. Weird, but that's just how it is. You'll get the hang of it soon enough.

## Wire gauges

The diameters of the gauges are not the same from system to system, so it's important to know which system is being used to describe the wire in your project and the wire you need to buy. The chart below shows the differences between the systems.

| Gauge | AWG | SWG |
|-------|---------|---------|
| 16 | 1.29 mm | 1.63 mm |
| 18 | 1.02 mm | 1.22 mm |
| 20 | 0.81 mm | 0.91 mm |
| 22 | 0.64 mm | 0.71 mm |
| 24 | 0.51 mm | 0.56 mm |
| 26 | 0.40 mm | 0.46 mm |
| 28 | 0.32 mm | 0.38 mm |
| 30 | 0.26 mm | 0.32 mm |

**Wire gauge**

# Wrapping

# Confetti
## earrings

**Techniques**
crinkling
making wrapped loops

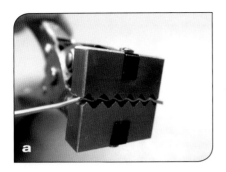
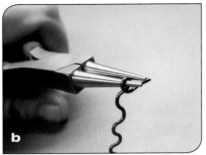
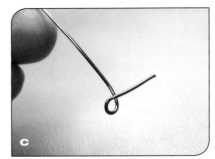

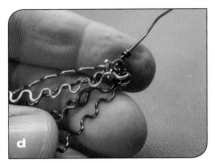

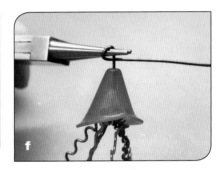

## Instructions

**1** Cut six pieces of wire in different lengths and colors.

**2** Crinkle the wires with different tightnesses using Zig-Zag parallel bending pliers **(a)**.

**3** Using roundnose pliers, make a 1¼" diameter plain loop at one end of each wire (Techniques, p. 10) **(b)**.

**4** Cut a 4" piece of wire.

**5** Use roundnose pliers to make the first half of a wrapped loop at one end of the wire. Make it large enough to accommodate six of the looped ends of the wires made in steps 1–3 **(c)**.

**6** String six wires on the loop and complete the wraps **(d)**.

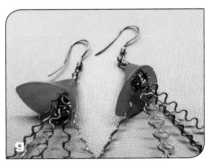

**7** String a tulip **(e)**.

**8** Make a wrapped loop (Techniques, p. 11) above the tulip **(f)**.

**9** Make a second earring dangle.

**10** Make a pair of matching earring wires (Techniques, p. 15). Attach one to each confetti dangle **(g)**.

## Materials
- 20-gauge colored wire in several colors
- **2** acrylic tulips

## Tools
- Basic Tool Kit
- Zig-Zag parallel bending pliers

# Portal
## pendant

**Techniques**
making a shepherd's
hook clasp
wrapping cord ends

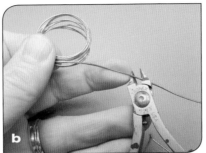

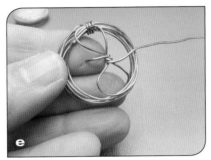
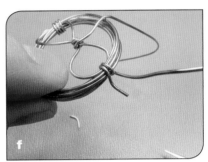

## Instructions

**1** Working from the spool of 18-gauge wire, wrap wire around the dowel several times, creating a "nest" **(a)**.

**2** Cut the wire, leaving a 2" tail **(b)**.

**3** Wrap the tail around the nested wires **(c)**.

**4** Pull two wires of the last loop in toward the middle with roundnose pliers forming an hourglass shape **(d)**.

**5** Cut a 6" piece of 18-gauge wire and tightly wrap the center of the hourglass together **(e)**.

**6** Cut a 6" piece of 18-gauge wire and coil it around the top of the wires, securing them together **(f)**.

## Materials
- 18-gauge colored wire
- Glass bead or round stone
- Leather cord

## Tools
- Basic Tool Kit
- Dowel (diameter equal to size of the glass bead)

**7** Position the bead in the wires and begin pulling wires over the bead to secure it in place **(g)**.

**8** Using the wire left over from the middle, wrap the end over and through the top **(h, i)**.

**9** Use roundnose pliers to bend and tighten the wires as needed to reduce slack **(j)**.

**10** Create a bail for your pendant from the remaining wire by making a wrapped loop (Techniques, p. 11) **(k)**.

**NOTE:**

Photo (l) shows the front of the pendant and photo (m) shows the back of the pendant.

**11** Using 18-gauge wire, wrap each end of the leather cord (Techniques, p. 11).

**12** Make a shepherd's hook to complete the clasp for the leather cord (Techniques, p. 13).

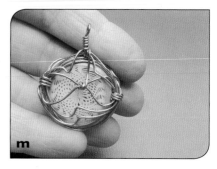

# Orange
## is the New Pink
## earrings

**Techniques**
adding beads
making earring wires

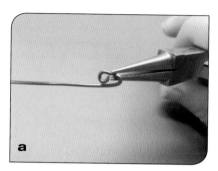

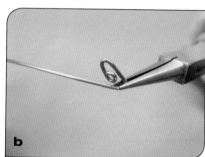

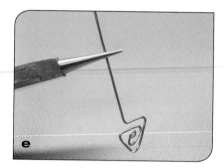

## Materials

- 18-gauge wire, orange
- 20-gauge wire, orange
- 24-gauge wire, gold
- **6** 4mm beads
- **2** earring wires (optional)

## Tools

- Basic Tool Kit

## Instructions

**1** Cut a 4" piece of 18-gauge wire.

**2** Using roundnose pliers, make a plain loop at one end of the wire (Techniques, p. 10).

**3** Grasp the wire just above the loop with your chainnose pliers and bend the wire 45 degrees **(a)**.

**4** Move your pliers slightly forward on the wire and make another 45-degree bend **(b)**.

**5** Continue making bends until you have a triangle with about a ¾" diameter **(c)**.

**6** Make a 90-degree bend in the wire positioned in the center of the triangle **(d)**.

**7** Using your roundnose pliers, grasp the wire about 1½" above the triangle **(e)**.

**8** Make a wrapped loop (Techniques, p. 11) **(f)**.

**9** Cut a 6" piece of 24-gauge wire.

**10** Wrap a coil starting at the base of the wrapped loop **(g)**.

**11** String a bead on 24-gauge wire.

**12** Wrap the 24-gauge wire around the 18-gauge wire three times **(h)**.

**13** String a second bead and coil the wire three times **(i)**.

**14** Repeat step 13 **(j)**.

**15** Make a second earring the mirror image of the first.

**16** Make your own earring wires and attach to the dangles (Techniques, p. 15) or attach purchased earring wires to the dangles **(k)**.

f

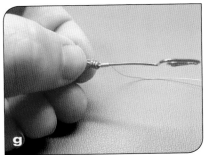

g

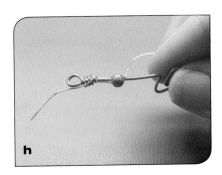

h

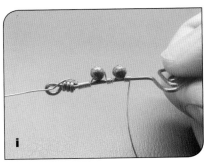

i

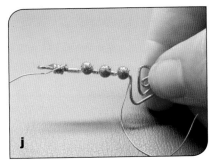

j

k

# Chrysalis
## earrings

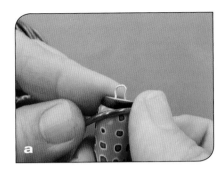

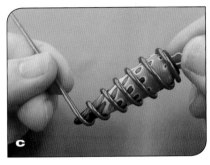

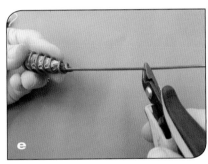

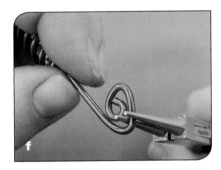

## Materials

- 12-gauge colored wire
- 20-gauge colored wire
- **2** tapered beads
- **2** earring wires (optional)

## Tools

- Basic Tool Kit

## Instructions

**1** Cut a 12" piece of 12-gauge aluminum wire.

**2** With your non-dominant hand, hold the end of the wire tightly to the top of the bead **(a)**.

**3** Gently begin coiling the wire from the top down in a loose spiral towards the bottom of the bead **(b, c)**.

**4.** Make a tight loop around the bottom of the bead and close **(d)**.

**5** Flush cut the wire about 2" below the end of the bead **(e)**.

**6** Use roundnose pliers to make a spiral at the bottom of the wire, spiraling up to the bottom of the bead **(f)**.

**7** Make a second earring.

**8** Make two earring wires from 20-gauge wire and attach to the top of each bead (Techniques, p. 15) or attach purchased earrings wires to the tops of each bead.

# Soft-Spoken
## bracelet

**Techniques**
· · · · · · · · · ·
using jump rings
· · · · · · · · · ·
making an S-hook
clasp

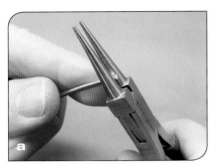

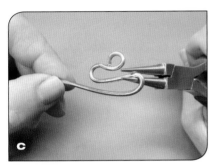

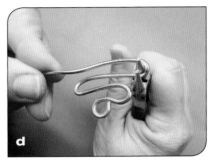

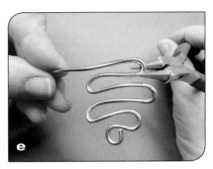

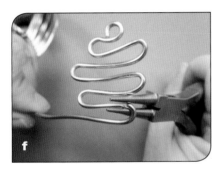

## Instructions

**1** Working from a spool of wire, make a loop at the end of the wire with the largest part of the roundnose pliers **(a)**.

**2** Move your pliers down the wire one plier width and bend the wire back, parallel to the remaining wire extending from the loop **(b)**.

**3** Position the pliers one plier width past the loop above and bend the wire back, parallel with the previous bend **(c)**.

**4** Move the pliers one width over from the end of the previous bend and bend the wire back, parallel to the top loop. This is creating a switch-back pattern **(d)**.

**5** Repeat as above, but this time, move the pliers in one width, making the next pass smaller than the previous one **(e)**.

**6** Make a second pass making the loops smaller by one plier width **(f)**.

## Materials

- 12-gauge aluminum wire (in three different colors or three variations of the same color)

## Tools

- Basic Tool Kit
- Anvil or bench block
- Domed chasing hammer

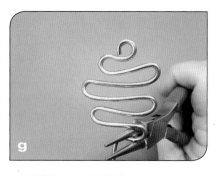

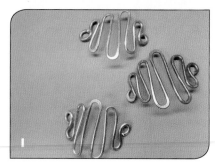

**7** Center your pliers below the previous pass and make a right-angle bend **(g)**.

**8** Make a plain loop **(h)**.

**9** Cut the component from the spool of wire **(i)**.

**10** Hammer the bends of the component using a domed chasing hammer with an anvil or bench block **(j)**.

**11** Gently curve the component with your fingers **(k)**.

**12** Make two more switch-back components using 12-gauge wire **(l)**.

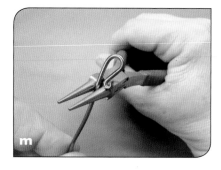

**13** Make a large S-hook clasp (Techniques, p. 12) **(m)**.

**14** Make four 9mm jump rings (Techniques, p. 12) **(n)**.

**15** Attach the components (including the clasp) with the jump rings. Attach a jump ring to the end of the bracelet opposite the clasp **(o, p)**.

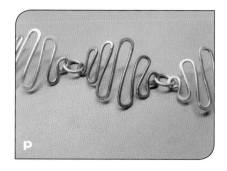

# Inner Beauty
## earrings

**Techniques**

making a bail

making integrated
earring wires

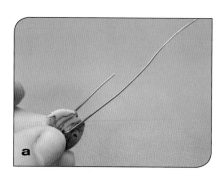

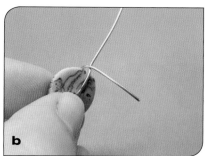

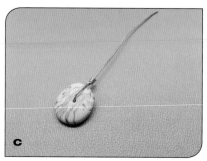

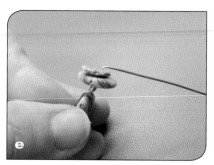

## Materials

- 20-gauge colored wire
- **6** center-drilled flat beads in decreasing sizes, two of each size

## Tools

- Basic Tool Kit
- 9mm dowel
- Anvil or bench block
- Domed chasing hammer
- Wire rounder

## Instructions

**1** Cut a 10" piece of wire.

**2** String the wire through the center of the largest bead, leaving about 1" on one side and about 9" on the opposite side.

**3** Bend both ends of the wire up and parallel with the bead **(a)**.

**4** Bend the short wire across the long wire above the bead **(b)**.

**5** Wrap the short wire around the long wire **(c)**.

**6** String the middle-size bead and then the smallest bead above the wire wrap **(d)**.

**7** Make a 90-degree bend over the top of the beads **(e)**.

**8** Position the chainnose pliers even with the edge of the middle-size bead and bend the wire 45 degrees **(f)**.

**9** Place a 9mm dowel next to the wire and pull the end of the wire up and over the dowel **(g)**.

**10** Repeat steps 1–9 to make a second earring.

**11** Cut the wire ends on each earring even using flush wire cutters **(h)**. Use a wire rounder to smooth each end.

**12** Use a domed chasing hammer with an anvil or bench block to hammer the front of each earring wire **(i)**.

**13** These are the completed earrings **(j)**.

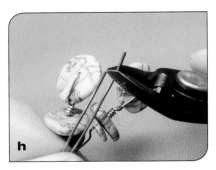

# How It All Began
## ring

Techniques
- shaping wire
- spiraling wire

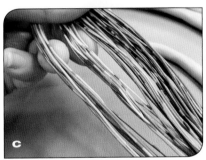

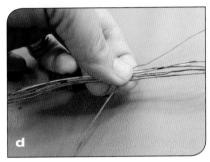

## Materials
- Vintage telephone wire (or 18-gauge wire in various colors)

## Tools
- Basic Tool Kit

## Instructions

**1** Strip the plastic coating off the vintage telephone wire **(a)**.

**2** If mounting ends are still attached to the wires, cut them off with flush wire cutters **(b)**.

**3** Choose six pieces and cut to 18" **(c)**.

**4** Choose an exterior ring color. Cut 1 yd. of this color.

**5** Begin in the middle of the bundle of six. Center the 1-yd. length of wire across the bundle **(d)**.

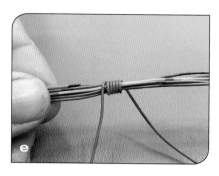

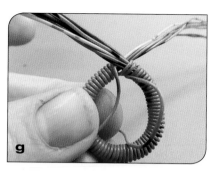

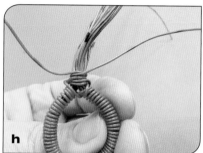

**6** Coil in one direction for half the distance of the finished ring (i.e. 1" for a size 7) **(e)**.

**7** Repeat on other side of the coil **(f)**.

**8** When the coiled section is the size you need, bring the two ends together to cross at the top.

**9** Wrap one end around the bundle on the opposite side two times. Repeat with the other end **(g)**.

**10** Bring all the bundled wire ends together. Wrap one end of the wire from step 9 around the double-bundle to the right and the other end around the double-bundle to the left **(h)**.

**11** Incorporate the remaining wire in the double-bundle **(i)**.

**12** Spread the wires **(j)**.

**13** Starting with the wires closest to the ring shank, use roundnose pliers to spiral each wire "in" toward the shank **(k)**.

**14** Continue spiraling the wires until all wires are completed **(l)**.

**15** Adjust the spirals and your ring is ready **(m)**.

# Bold and Colorful
## bracelet

**Techniques**
· · · · · · · · ·
making a shepherd's
hook clasp
· · · · · · · · · ·
using jump rings

**TIP**

12-gauge aluminum wire is
very light and soft. It can be
manipulated into a variety of
shapes, easily. By closing the
shapes, the soft wire is able
to maintain its form.

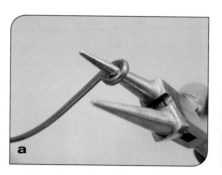

## Materials

- 12-gauge aluminum wire in a variety of colors
- 18-gauge aluminum wire in a variety of colors
- 26-gauge aluminum wire in a variety of colors

## Tools

- Basic Tool Kit
- Wrap 'n' Tap pliers

## Instructions

**1** Working from the spool, use roundnose pliers to make a small loop at the end of one colored wire **(a)**. Repeat in a second color.

**2** Using your non-dominant hand to hold the loop, gently guide the wire with your dominant hand around to form a 1½" open spiral **(b)**. Flush cut the end and make a ¼" loop. Repeat in a second color **(c)**.

**3** Make a triangle (out of a different color wire) by making a loop at the end of the wire, moving roundnose pliers slightly up from the center loop and pulling the wire into a 45-degree angle. Move up again and repeat. Continue until you have a triangle about 1½" in diameter. Flush cut the ends and and make a loop **(d)**.

**4** Repeat the process you used to make the triangle, only make 90-degree turns each time you move your roundnose pliers. Flush cut the ends and make a loop **(e)**.

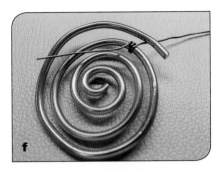

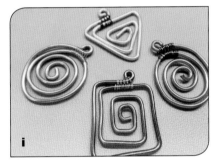

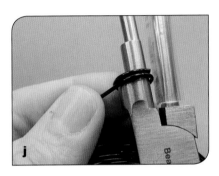

**5** With 8" of 26-gauge colored wire, use roundnose pliers to wrap the ends of each closed shape. Make the first two wraps around the inside wire **(f)**.

**6** Make two wraps around the outer wire. Now make two wraps around the inside wire **(g)**. Repeat, alternating wraps on the inside and outside wires until you are near the end of the outer wire.

**7** Make a loop at the end using the roundnose pliers **(h)**.

**8** Repeat with each shape **(i)**.

**9** Using the large barrel of the Wrap 'n' Tap pliers, make 10 jump rings from 18-gauge wire (Techniques, p. 12) **(j)**.

**10** Cut the jump rings apart with your wire cutters **(k)**.

**11** Using roundnose pliers, open a jump ring. Attach the spiral components to each other with two jump rings **(l, m)**.

**12** Using 18-gauge wire, make a shepherd's hook **(n)**. (Techniques, p. 13). Attach to one end of the bracelet with two jump rings.

**13** Push out the sections of each spiral shape to add dimension to your bracelet **(o)**.

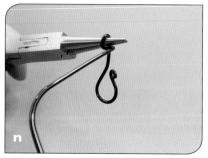

**14** Add two jump rings to the last spiral to complete the bracelet clasp **(p)**.

# Sacré Bleu
## earrings

**Techniques**
· · · · · · · · · ·
making plain loops
· · · · · · · · · ·
making wrapped
loops

## Materials

- 20-gauge wire in three colors
- **6** accent beads
- **4** spacer beads
- **2** dangle crystals, beads, or charms
- **2** focal beads

## Tools

- Basic Tool Kit
- Anvil or bench block
- Wire rounder
- Wrap 'n' Tap pliers

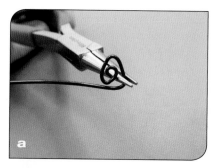

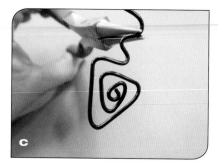

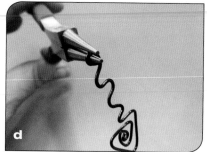

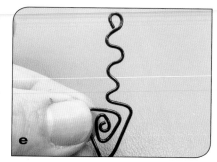

## Instructions

**1** Using roundnose pliers, make a plain loop (Techniques, p. 10) at one end of the wire.

**2** Place chainnose pliers at the end of the loop and make a straight bend a pliers' length long, forming a triangle. Move again and repeat **(a)**.

**3** In the center of the last side of the triangle, use chainnose pliers to make a 45-degree bend in the wire to center the post **(b)**.

**4** Moving in small increments and using the pliers' jaw as a guide, make a series of zig-zag bends in the wire **(c)**.

**5** At the end of the wire, make a plain loop using roundnose pliers **(d, e)**.

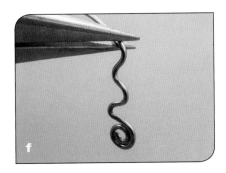

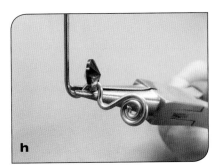

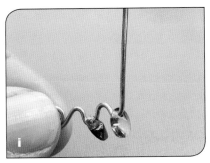

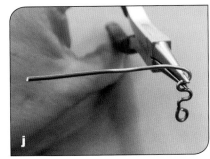

**6** With a second color of wire, make a two-loop spiral **(f)**.

**7** Use chainnose pliers to make three zig-zag bends above the spiral **(g)**.

**8** String an accent bead and then bend the wire behind the bead to continue the zig-zag pattern **(h)**.

**9** Repeat step 8 **(i)**.

**10** Choose a third color of wire. Make a plain loop at one end and make three zig-zag bends above the loop **(j)**.

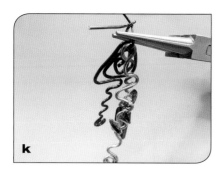

**11** Open the plain loop. Add a dangle and close the loop.

**12** Make the first half of a wrapped loop with a piece of 20-gauge wire. String the decorative wires and complete the wraps **(k, l)**.

**13** String a spacer bead, a focal bead, and a spacer bead above the wraps **(m)**.

**14** Using roundnose pliers, bend the wire 45 degrees directly above the last spacer bead **(n)**.

**15** Place the wire in Wrap 'n' Tap pliers as far into the jaw as you can get and as close to the spacer bead as possible **(o)**.

**16** Pull the wire up and over the large barrel to form the earring wire **(p)**.

**17** Remove the earring from the pliers and gently bend back the bottom of the wire **(q)**.

**18** With a domed chasing hammer, gently tap the front curve of the earring wire on the anvil or bench block **(r)**.

**19** Make a second earring the mirror image of the first.

**20** Use a wire rounder on the earring wire ends.

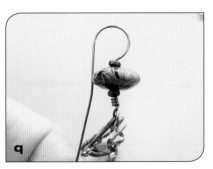

Coiling

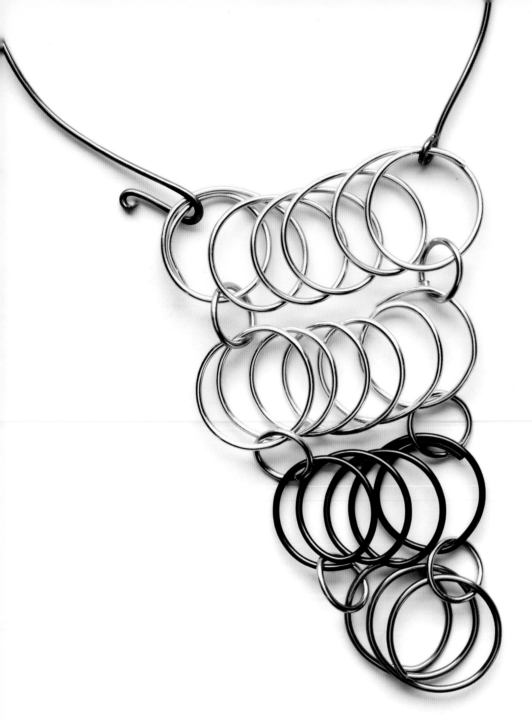

Techniques
• • • • • • • •
sculpting coils
• • • • • • • •
making a custom
neck wire

# Loop-T-Loop
## necklace

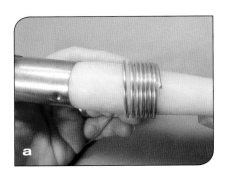

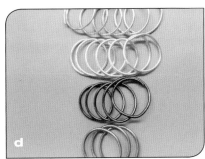

## Materials

- 12-gauge aluminum wire in four varied colors

## Tools

- Basic Tool Kit
- 9mm dowel or other small mandrel
- Anvil or bench block
- Coffee can or other large mandrel
- Domed chasing hammer
- Wrap 'n' Tap pliers

## Instructions

**1** Find a dowel or other round object for the size of loops you would like to make (a prescription pill bottle is a good size).

**2** Working from a spool of wire, wrap the wire six times around the small mandrel. Trim the coil from the spool **(a)**.

**3** Pull the coil off of the mandrel and gently spread the loops apart **(b)**.

**4** Continue to spread the loops apart until the spacing is what you desire for the largest link of your necklace **(c)**.

**5** Repeat steps 1–4 three times with different colored wire. Make each coil one loop smaller than the previous link **(d)**.

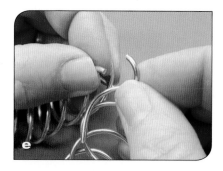

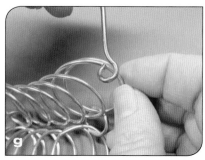

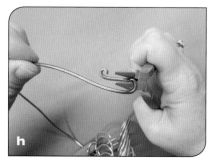

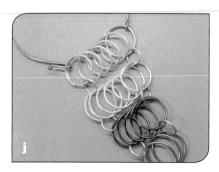

**TIP**

**You can achieve a different look by making the same number of loops, but leaving the loops a bit tighter when you pull them off the mandrel.**

**6** Make six jump rings using the large barrel of the Wrap 'n' Tap pliers or a 9mm dowel (Techniques, p.12).

**7** Attach each coil section in descending size with the jump rings **(e)**.

**8** Cut an 18" piece of wire.

**9** Using a coffee can or other large mandrel, shape the wire into a neck wire. Check the fit and adjust if necessary **(f)**.

**10** Make a plain loop at one end of the wire (Techniques, p. 10) and attach it to one side of the coiled component **(g)**.

**11** Using roundnose pliers, make a closed shepherd's hook on the opposite end of the wire (Techniques, p. 13) **(h)**.

**12** Hammer the end of the hook using a domed chasing hammer with an anvil or bench block **(i)**.

**13** Attach the hook to the opposite side of the coil as a clasp **(j)**.

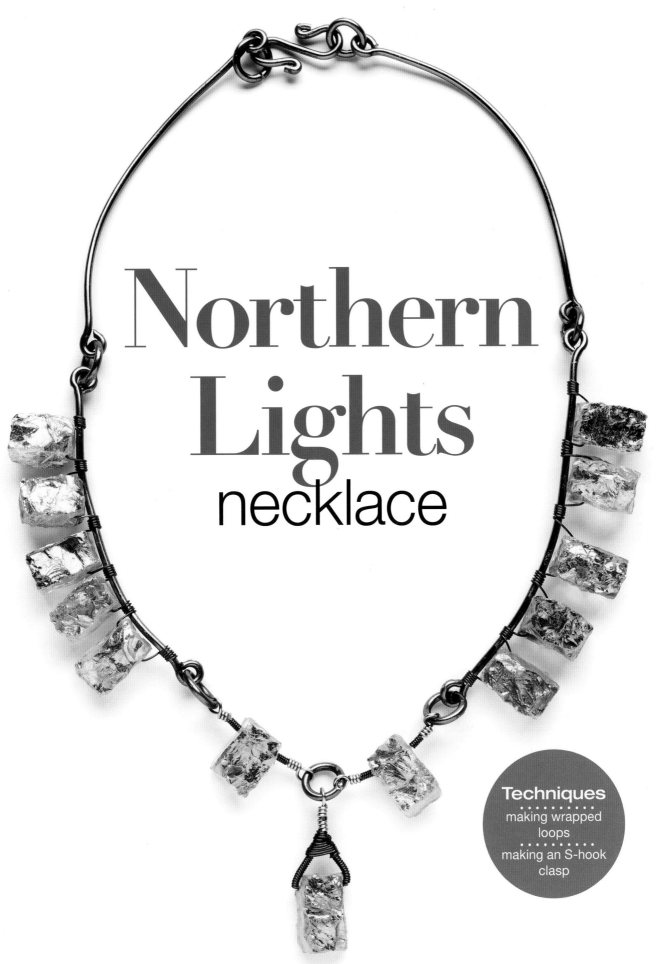

# Northern Lights
## necklace

**Techniques**
........
making wrapped
loops
........
making an S-hook
clasp

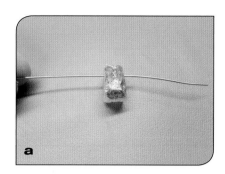

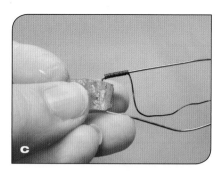

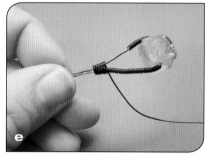

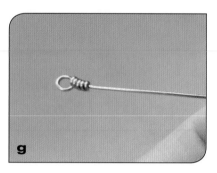

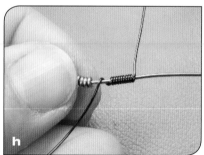

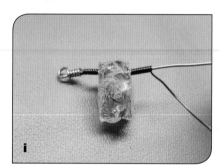

## Materials

- 12-gauge colored wire
- 18-gauge colored wire
- 20-gauge colored wire
- 24-gauge colored wire
- **13** top-drilled beads

## Tools

- Basic Tool Kit
- Anvil or bench block
- Domed chasing hammer
- Wrap 'n' Tap pliers or 9mm wooden dowel

## Instructions

### Pendant

**1** Cut a 6" piece of 24-gauge wire and string it through a top-drilled bead **(a)**.

**2** Position your bead in the middle of the wire. Bend both ends of the wire parallel with the sides of the bead **(b)**.

**3** Using your 24-gauge wire, make a ¼" coil on each side of the wire **(c)**.

**4** Pull both wires together. Using both ends of the 24-gauge wire, begin wrapping the two 18-gauge ends together **(d)**.

**5** Bend one 18-gauge wire down and make a wrapped coil around the remaining 18-gauge wire **(e)**.

**6** Using roundnose pliers, make a 3mm loop with one of the wires. Take that wire and make three coils going down. Wrap the other wire in the same manner, but making the three coils going up. When both meet they will form one coil. **(f)**.

**7** Cut a piece of 20-gauge wire 5" long. Make a wrapped loop at one end of the wire (Techniques, p. 11) **(g)**.

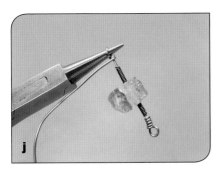

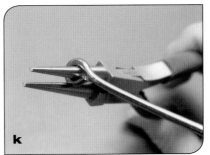

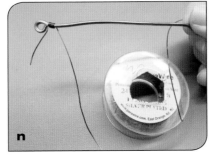

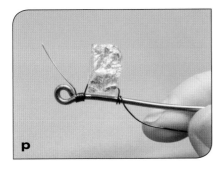

**8** Using 24-gauge wire, coil the wire five times around the 20-gauge wire **(h)**.

**9** Thread both wires through the hole in a bead. Then, using the 24-gauge wire, coil the wire five times around the 20-gauge wire **(i)**.

**10** Make a wrapped loop at this end of the wire **(j)**. Cut off the excess wire and tuck in the ends.

**11** Repeat steps 7–10 to make a second connector for the pendant.

**Necklace**

**1** Cut a 10" piece of 12-gauge wire.

**2** Make a plain loop at each end of the wire with the 9mm dowel or the medium barrel of your Wrap 'n' Tap pliers (Techniques, p. 10) **(k)**.

**3** Bend the neck of each loop so the loops lie parallel with the wire **(l)**.

**4** Gently form the wire with your fingers **(m)**.

**5** Cut a 36" piece of 24-gauge wire. Make a plain loop at one end of the wire. Using 24-gauge wire, coil the wire five times around the 12-gauge wire **(n)**.

**6** Thread the wire through the hole in a bead **(o)**.

**7** Bring the wire back up to the 12-gauge wire and coil around it five times **(p)**.

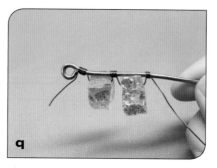

**8** Continue with all of your beads **(q)**.

**9** Make seven 12-gauge jump rings using your Wrap 'n' Tap pliers (Techniques, p. 12)

**10** Cut two 8" pieces of 12-gauge wire.

**11** Make a loop at the end of each wire with the middle barrel of your Wrap 'n' Tap pliers. Gently form the wires with your fingers to complete the necklace shape **(r)**.

**12** Using a jump ring, attach a beaded component to one side of the necklace-shaped wire **(s)**.

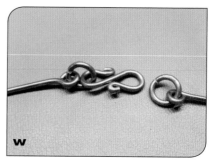

**13** Repeat with the second side of the necklace-shaped wire **(t)**.

**14** Attach the end of each beaded component with a jump ring to the pendant connection **(u)**.

**15** Attach the three components with one of the jump rings **(v)**.

**16** Attach the last two jump rings to the ends to hold the clasp of the pendant.

**17** Make an S-hook clasp with 12-gauge wire (Techniques, p. 12). Attach it to the necklace wire with a jump ring **(w)**.

# Northern Lights
## earrings

**Techniques**

making integrated
earring wires

making coiled
beads

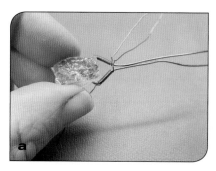

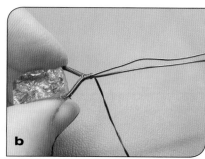

## Materials

- 20-gauge colored wire
- 24-gauge colored wire
- **2** top-drilled beads

## Tools

- Basic Tool Kit
- Wrap 'n' Tap pliers or 9mm wooden dowel

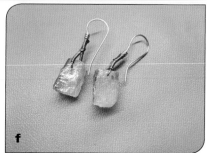

## Instructions

**1** Cut a 6" piece of 20-gauge wire and string a top-drilled bead.

**2** Center the bead on the wire. Bend both ends of the wire parallel with the sides of the bead.

**3** Using 24-gauge wire, make a ¼" coil on each side of the bead around the 20-gauge wire **(a)**.

**4** Pull both wires together and using both ends of the 24-gauge wire, wrap the 18-gauge ends together for about ¼" **(b)**.

**5** Bend one 18-gauge wire down and wrap a coil around the remaining 18-gauge wire **(c)**.

**6** Trim the wire tail with flush wire cutters.

**7** Position the Wrap 'n' Tap pliers or dowel just above the coil and tilt the wire back 45 degrees **(d)**.

**8** To form an earring wire, bend the wire up and over the dowel and down towards the coiled wire **(e)**.

**9** Make a second earring the mirror image of the first **(f)**.

# Bold & Bitters
## earrings

**TIP**

The advantage of aluminum wire for earrings is that it is so light. Any other metal in 12-gauge would be too heavy for this design.

## Materials

- 12-gauge aluminum wire
- 18-gauge aluminum wire
- 24-gauge aluminum wire
- **2** beads with 3mm holes
- **2** earring wires (optional)

## Tools

- Basic Tool Kit
- 1.25mm hand punch
- 4mm bail-making pliers
- Anvil or bench block
- Domed chasing hammer

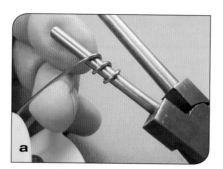

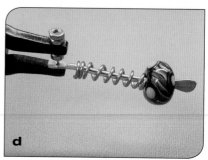

## Instructions

**1** Cut two 1½" pieces of 12-gauge wire.

**2** Trim both ends of each wire with flush wire cutters.

**3** Using a smooth hammer face and anvil surface, strike one end of each wire several times to flatten.

**TIP**
Aluminum wire is very soft and the color is only on the surface of the metal, so some of the color may come off.

**4** String a bead onto the paddled wire.

**5** Use bailing pliers to make a coil from a piece of 18-gauge wire. Spiral the wire six times, leaving about a ⅛" space between each loop **(a)**.

**6** After the sixth twist, make the next revolution tight **(b)**. Remove the coil from the bailing pliers and string it on the 12-gauge wire above the bead.

**7** Using a smooth hammer face and anvil surface, strike the end of the wire several times to flatten **(c)**.

**8** Punch a hole in the top paddle using a 1.25mm hand punch **(d)**.

**9** Repeat steps 4–8 to make a second earring.

**10** Make your own earring wires (Techniques, p. 15) or attach purchased earring wires to the two earring components.

# Red Splatter
## bracelet

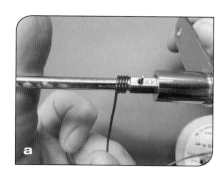

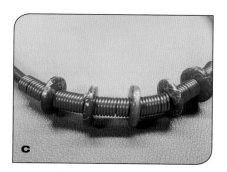

## Materials

- 18-gauge colored wire
- **7** donut beads with 5mm holes
- 5mm diameter leather cord

## Tools

- Basic Tool Kit
- Anvil or bench block
- Domed chasing hammer
- Mister Twister coil maker or 5mm wooden dowel
- Scissors

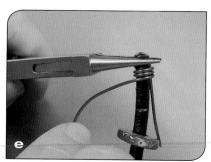

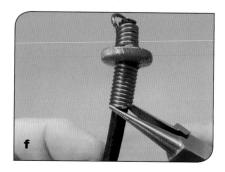

## Instructions

**1** Using the Mister Twister (or a wooden dowel), make eight 10-wrap coils **(a)**.

**2** Cut a 7" piece of 5mm leather.

**3** String a coil, a bead, and a coil on the leather **(b)**.

**4** Continue the pattern until you have five beads and six coils. Center the beads and coils **(c)**.

**5** Using chainnose pliers, pinch the end of each wire into the leather **(d)**.

**6** String a coil and a bead on each end of the leather.

**7** Wrap each leather cord end (Techniques, p. 11) **(e)**.

**8** Push the bead and coil down towards the wrapped end of the leather and pinch the last wire into the leather **(f)**.

**9** Make a shepherd's hook clasp (Techniques, p. 13) and attach it to the end of the bracelet.

# Blue Fish
## earrings

**Techniques**
· · · · · · · · · ·
making coiled beads
· · · · · · · · · ·
making wrapped
loops

**TIP**
Creating different kinds of
dangles on each earring
makes this project a bit
more fun.

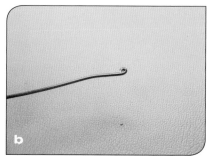

## Materials

- 18-gauge colored wire
- 24-gauge colored wire
- **10** spacer beads
- **5** disk beads
- **1** accent bead
- **2** earring wires (optional)

## Tools

- **Basic Tool Kit**
- Wrap 'n' Tap pliers

## Instructions

### Earring Base

**1** Make four four six-coil "beads" by wrapping 24-gauge wire over a piece of 18-gauge wire.

**2** Make a wrapped loop on one end of the wire (Techniques, p. 11). String a spacer bead, a disk bead, a spacer bead, a coil, a spacer bead, a disk bead, and a spacer bead onto a piece of 18-gauge wire to finish the base. **(a)**.

**3** Make a second base.

### Earring Component #1

**4** Make a very tight pinch at one end of a piece of 18-gauge wire **(b)**.

**5** String a spacer bead, a disk bead, a spacer bead, and a coil onto the wire. String the end through a loop of one of the earring bases **(c)** and make a wrapped loop **(d)**.

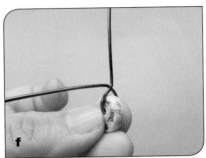

**Earring Component #2**

**6** Center a disk bead on an 18-gauge wire and bend the wires parallel to each other.

**7** Cross the wires to form an "X" above the disk bead **(e)**.

**8** Bend the wires into a right angle **(f)**.

**9** Make a set of wraps above the disk using the horizontal wire **(g)**.

**10** String a coil and the loop of the second earring base. Make a wrapped loop **(h, i)**.

**11** Make your own earring wires (Techniques, p. 15) or attach purchased earring wires to the two earring components.

# Blue Fish
## bracelet

**Techniques**
· · · · · · · · · ·
making wrpped loops
· · · · · · · · · ·
making a hook clasp

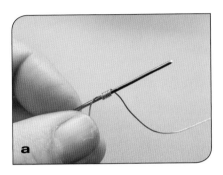

## Materials

- 18-gauge colored wire
- 24-gauge colored wire
- **12** spacer beads
- 1mm round bead
- **5** 1mm ceramic square beads (or other beads)
- Toggle bead

## Tools

- Basic Tool Kit
- Wrap 'n' Tap pliers

## Instructions

**1** Make eight six-coil "beads" by wrapping 24-gauge wire over a piece of 18-gauge wire dowel **(a)**. Each completed coil "bead" will be about ⅛" long.

**2** String a coil, a spacer, a square, and a spacer. Repeat this pattern until you have strung six coil beads, 10 spacer beads, and five square beads on about 5" of 18-gauge wire **(b)**.

**3** Make a wrapped loop on each end of the piece of wire (Techniques, p. 11) **(c)**.

**4** On a 5" piece of 18-gauge wire, string a coil, a round bead, and a coil. Make a wrapped loop on each end **(d)**.

**5** Slightly curve each of the components to accommodate the shape of your wrist.

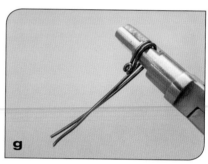

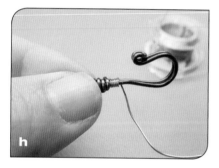

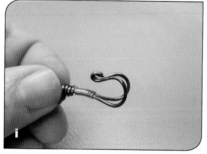

**6** Use 18-gauge wire and Wrap 'n' Tap pliers on the small barrel to make three jump rings.

**7** Attach the two components with one of the jump rings **(e)**.

**8** Use Wrap 'n' Tap pliers to make two large jump rings. Use both to attach your toggle component **(f)**.

**9** Cut a 6" piece of 18-gauge wire to make a hook for your bracelet.

**10** Fold the wire in half to make a basic hook **(g)**.

**11** Embellish the hook with the 24-gauge wire **(h)**.

**12** Separate the wires of the hook **(i)**.

**13** Attach the hook to the end of the bracelet with a small jump ring **(j)**.

# Beach Comber's
## bracelet

**Techniques**
· · · · · · · · · · · · ·
making a toggle
clasp

making wrapped
loops

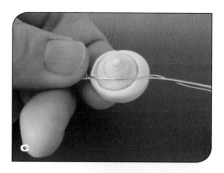

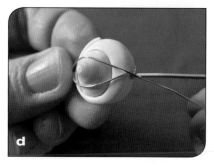

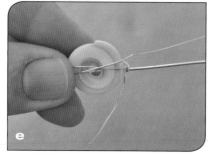

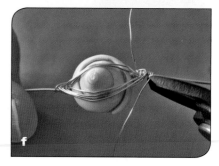

## Materials

- 20-gauge colored wire
- 26-gauge coloed wire
- **22** drilled seashells (or other beads)
- 1.25mm coral or other rectangle-shaped objects
- 1.25mm loop-shaped object

## Tools

- Basic Tool Kit

# Instructions

### Bracelet chain

**1** Cut a 3" piece of 26-gauge wire. Make a wrapped loop at the end of the wire (Techniques, p. 11). String a shell on the wire and make a wrapped loop above the shell **(a)**.

**2** Cut a second piece of wire. (The length is dependent on the size of your shell or bead.)

**3** Connect the loops to each other. Repeat step 1 to make a total of three strands of shells the length needed to form the chain part of the bracelet **(b).**

### TIP

Add wraps to a few shell links, if desired. (My bracelet has two dark shells that are wrapped.) Cut a 6" piece of 20-gauge wire and center a shell on the wire. Working off a spool of 26-gauge wire, wrap once around the 20-gauge

wire and then bring the 26-gauge wire across the front of the centered shell (c).

Wrap the 26-gauge wire around the 20-gauge wire at the other side of the shell, once. Bring the wire across the front of the shell again, moving in a clockwise direction (d). You can also add a few wraps behind the shell to hold it in place, if necessary (e).

Wrap the 26-gauge wire below the first wrap, once. Continue moving around the shell, wrapping once on each side for as many times is desired (f).

Wrap one last tight coil and cut off the excess wire. Make a wrapped loop on each end of the link to connect it to the chain.

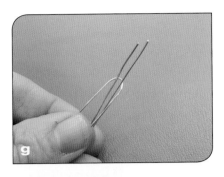

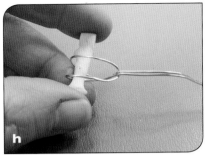

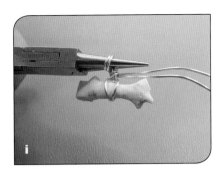

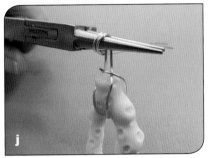

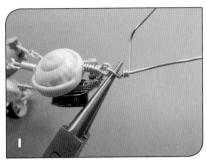

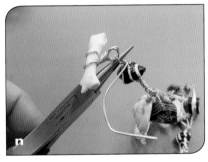

### Toggle

**4** Bend about 8" of 20-gauge wire in half. Thread the ends of the wire through the wire loop **(g)**.

**5** Place the piece of coral (to be used as the toggle bar) in the double loop **(h)**.

**6** Cinch the wires tightly against the coral.

**7** Make a wrapped loop using the wire ends as one **(i)**.

**8** Repeat steps 5 and 6 for a second piece of coral. Thread the wire through the opening of the coral and then thread the ends of the wire back through the loop in the wire **(j, k)**.

### Finishing

**9** Now make a wrapped loop fastening all of the chains to the one wire **(l)**.

**10** Put a small shell on the wire and string the three chains. Now, make a wrapped loop incorporating the toggle bar **(m)**.

**11** Hook the three chains on the opposite end together with a wrapped loop of 20-gauge wire. String a small shell and make a wrapped loop incorporating the other half of the toggle bar **(n)**.

**12** Your seashell bracelet is now complete **(o)**.

### TIP

I found the perfect pieces of coral for a toggle, however, you can use a commercial toggle.

# Beach Comber's
## earrings

**Techniques**
making plain loops
making earring wires

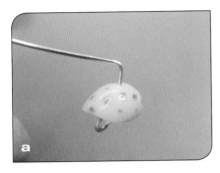

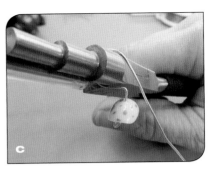

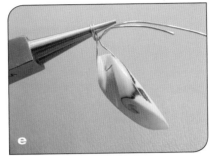

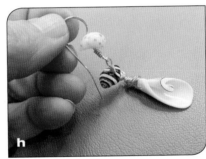

## Materials

- 20-gauge colored wire
- 26-gauge colored wire
- **4** small seashells
- **2** top-drilled seashells
- **2** earring wires (optional)

## Tools

- Basic Tool Kit
- Wire rounder
- Wrap 'n' Tap pliers

## Instructions

**1** Cut a 3" piece of 20-gauge wire and make a plain loop at one end (Techniques, p. 10).

**2** String a small seashell on the wire and bend the wire 90 degrees over the shell, leaving a ¼" gap **(a)**.

**3** Position the wire on the large barrel of Wrap 'n' Tap pliers, making sure the shell is up against the rubber covered barrel **(b)**.

**4** Pull the wire up and over the metal barrel until it is touching the seashell **(c)**.

**5** Cut a 12" piece of 26-gauge wire. Thread 3" of the wire through a top- drilled seashell **(d)**.

**6** Position roundnose pliers above the shell and make the first half of a wrapped loop **(e)**.

**7** Wrap the wire down to the shell and start back up toward the pliers **(f)**. Wrap until you like the number of wraps and then trim the wire.

**8** Cut a 3–5" piece of 20-gauge wire. Make the first half of a wrapped loop and connect the

top-drilled dangle. Complete the wraps and trim the wire **(g)**.

**9** String a seashell and make the first half of a wrapped loop. Use the remaining length of wire as the earring wire (Techniques, p. 15).

**10** Trim. Use a wire rounder to smooth the ends **(h)**.

**11** Make a second earring to match the first.

# Pacific Blue
## earrings

**Techniques**
· · · · · · · · · ·
making a plain loop
· · · · · · · · · ·
making a coiled spacer

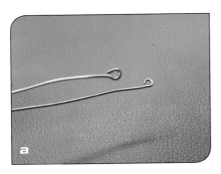

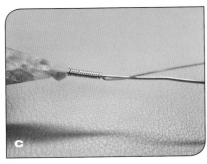

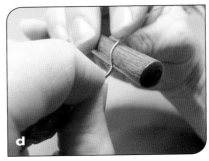

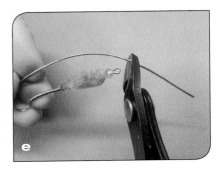

## Instructions

**1** Cut two, 8" pieces of 20-gauge wire.

**2** Make a plain loop at one end of each (Techniques, p. 10) **(a)**.

**3** String a bicone, a gemstone, and a bicone on each wire **(b)**.

**4** Coil 1" of 24-gauge wire directly onto each wire above the bicone **(c)**.

**5** Position the dowel above the end of one coil and bend the wire back 45 degrees **(d)**.

**6** Gently curl the wire all the way back to the loop with your fingers. Trim the excess wire with flush wire cutters **(e)**. Use a wire rounder to smooth the end.

**7** Repeat steps 5 and 6 with the second earring.

**8** Hook the end of the wire through the plain loop when the earrings are worn.

## Materials
- 20-gauge colored wire
- 24-gauge colored wire
- **4** 4mm bicone crystals
- **2** 1.5mm oval gemstone beads

## Tools
- Basic Tool Kit
- ¼" Dowel
- Wire rounder

# Mardi Gras
## bracelet

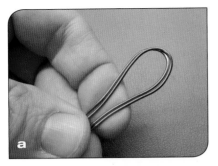

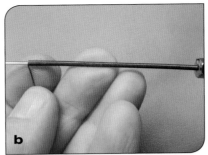

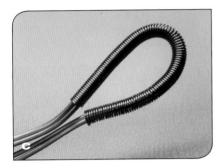

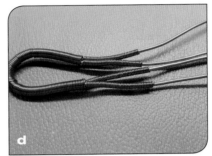

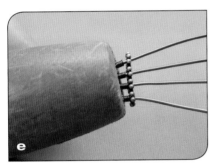

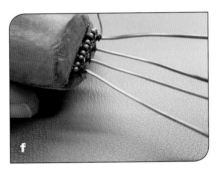

## Instructions

**1** Cut two 10" pieces of 18-gauge wire.

**2** Loosely fold the wires in half **(a)**.

**3** Using a Mister Twister (or 2mm wooden dowel), make a 2" coil from 26-gauge wire **(b)**.

**4** Slide the coil over both wires and center it in the middle of the bend **(c)**.

**5** Cut two 4" pieces of 26-gauge wire and make one ½" coil with each.

**6** String one coil on each wire **(d)**.

**7** Pick up one four-hole spacer bar **(e)**. Secure the wired section with a ring clamp so you can keep the spacing consistent (and keep your fingers from cramping as you work). Create a 1" over/under weave using 26-gauge wire in a different color than your frame **(f)**. (See next page.)

(See next page.)

## Materials
- 18-gauge colored wire
- 26-gauge wire in two different colors
- **24** metallic spacer beads
- **6** four-hole spacer bars
- **4** 4mm cube shaped crystals

## Tools
- Basic Tool Kit
- Mister Twister wire coiler or 2mm wooden dowel
- Ring clamp
- Ruler

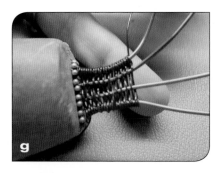
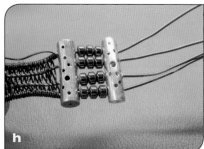

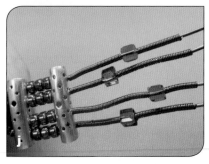
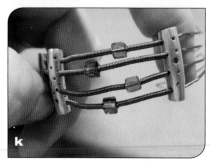

## Over/Under Weaving

**8a** The 26-gauge weaving wire travels under the first 18-gauge frame wire and then over the second 18-gauge frame wire. It continues under the third 18-gauge frame wire and over the fourth 18-gauge frame wire in an over/under pattern.

**8b** Make a loop around the fourth wire frame.

**8c** After the loop is pulled tight against the fourth wire frame, make a U-turn with the weaving wire and weave back to the first frame wire.

**8d** Now the 26-gauge weaving wire travels under the third wire frame and over the second wire frame, and loops around the first wire frame.

**8e** Make a U-turn with the wire and go under the first wire frame, over the second wire frame, under the third wire frame, and loop over the fourth wire frame. Repeat this pattern **(g)**.

**9** String one hole of a spacer bar, three spacer beads, and one hole of a spacer bar on each wire **(h)**.

**10** Working off of the spool of 26-gauge wire, make a 1½" coil for each wire.

**11** Cut the coils into staggered lengths **(i)**, but keep pairs together.

**12** String one piece of a coil, a crystal, and the paired piece of coil on each wire **(j)**. (The segments should be equal in length, but the crystals will be staggered.)

**13** String a spacer bar after the last coil is in place **(k)**.

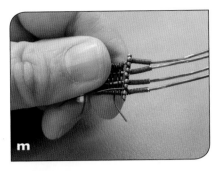 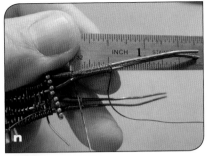 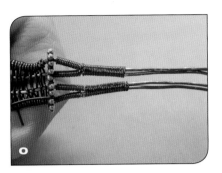

 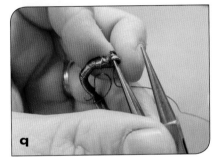 

**14** Complete the remainder of the bracelet by repeating steps 5–9 in reverse order (that is—starting with step number 9) **(l)**.

**15** Separate the wires after the last spacer bar and coil ½" of each of the four wires **(m)**.

**16** Pull the first and second wires together and coil around both for ½" **(n)**.

**17** Repeat step 16 for the third and fourth wires **(o)**.

**18** Pull the four wires together and continue to coil around them to the end of the wires **(p)**.

**19** Loop the ends up and over the last coils **(q)**.

**20** With roundnose pliers, bend the ends back to create a hook **(r)**.

# Mardi Gras earrings

**Techniques**
• • • • • • • • • •
making wrapped loops
• • • • • • • • • •
making earring wires

## Materials

• 20-gauge colored wire
• 26-gauge colored wire
• **6** 4mm accent beads
• **2** 6mm cube crystals
• **2** earring wires (optional)

## Tools

• Basic Tool Kit

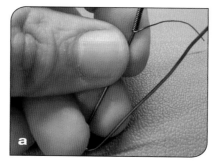

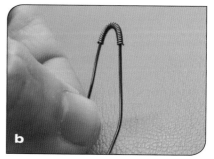

## Instructions

**1** Cut a 4" piece of 20-gauge wire.

**2** Fold the wire in half.

**3** With your hands, coil the 26-gauge wire onto the 20-gauge wire for ½" **(a)**.

**4** Slide the coil to the curve of the bend in the wire **(b)**.

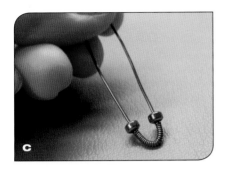

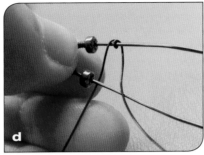

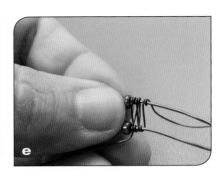

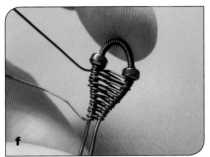

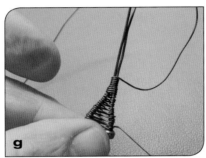

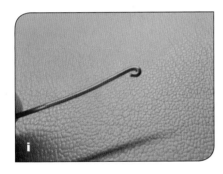

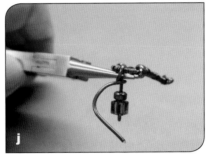

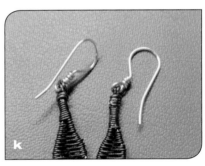

**5** String an accent bead on each side of the coil **(c)**.

**6** Make an over/under weave in a contrasting color of 26-gauge wire for ¾". Start the weave under the first wire, then loop two times around the second wire, coming up under the first wire in which you make two loops. Continue back across the second wire **(d)**.

**7** Gradually tighten your weave, bringing the wires closer together as you go **(e, f)**.

**8** Bring the two wires together into a single coil wrap **(g)**.

**9** Hold the two wires in your roundnose pliers, about 1¼" above the weave. Make a wrapped loop (Techniques, p. 11) **(h)**.

**10** Cut a 2" piece of wire the same color as the weave.

**11** Make a tight bend on one end **(i)**.

**12** String a crystal and an accent bead.

**13** Make a wrapped loop, connecting the dangle to the coiled loop at the bottom of the earring base before completing the wraps **(j)**.

**14** Make a second earring to match the first.

**15** Make your own earring wires (Techniques, p. 15) or attach purchased earring wires **(k)**.

# New Beginnings
## bracelet

**Techniques**
making Viking knit
making wire cones

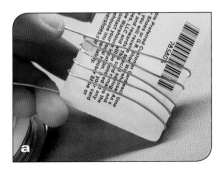

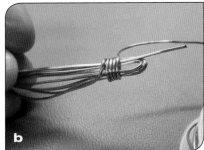

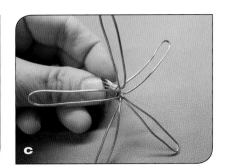

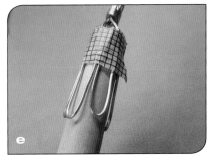

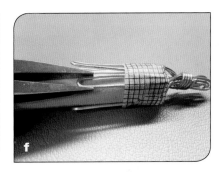

# Instructions

### Viking Knit

**1** Wrap the 18-gauge copper wire around the credit card five times—making five loose loops **(a)**. Slide the loops off of the card.

**2** Wrap the ends of the loops (that are still attached to the spool) in a tight coil **(b)** and cut away from the spool with flush cutters.

**3** Separate the loops, creating a "flower" shape **(c)**.

**4** Position the flower in the center of the ½" dowel and flatten the petals down the sides of the dowel. Make sure they are evenly spaced **(d)**.

**5** Tape the wire to the dowel so it doesn't slip while you are working **(e)**.

**6** Use flatnose pliers to pinch each of the petals. Separate them so they are equally spaced from each other **(f)**.

## Materials

- 12-gauge colored wire
- 18-gauge colored wire in two colors
- 24-gauge colored wire in two colors
- 26-gauge colored wire
- **10** 8mm rondelles
- **20** 3mm cube crystals
- **20** 3mm round beads

## Tools

- Basic Tool Kit
- ½" wooden dowel
- Credit card
- Draw plate
- Painter's tape

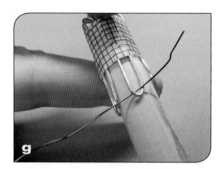

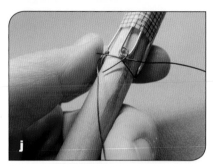

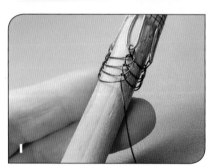

**7** Cut a 36" piece of 26-gauge wire from the spool. Starting on the left side of any loop, thread the wire through the loop, entering from the back **(g)**.

**8** Hold the loop end and cross the spool end of the wire over the long end of wire, creating a cursive "e" **(h)**.

**9** Hold the loop in place with the thumb of your non-dominant hand. Loop the end of the wire through the next loop, to the right of the first loop from the right side **(i)**. (This is opposite from how you started.)

**10** Make a cursive "e," holding the loop with the thumb of your non-dominant hand to prevent it from pulling tight **(j)**. Repeat this process until you get all the way around the dowel and are back at the first loop.

**11** Push your wire from the right side in behind the "x" made by the first loop **(k)**.

**12** Pull the wire, creating a loop similar to the one above. Continue all the way around, going in behind the "x" of the previous loop and holding it with the thumb of your non-dominant hand to secure the size **(l)**.

**13** Continue this process until you have a tube 3/4 of the length of your desired finished length **(m)**. (You can continue doing this on the dowel.)

**14** When you have the length of knit you need, cut it off the dowel **(n)**.

**TIP**
If you leave a section on the dowel, you can continue working with it for a new project. This way you do not have to go through the beginning process.

**15** Now the tube is ready to pull through the draw plate **(o)**.

**TIP**
I made my draw plate from a piece of wood, but you can purchase draw plates from any jewelry supply or hobby store (p).

**16** Start by pinching one side of the knit tube so it fits into the largest hole of your draw plate **(q)**.

**17** Thread a scrap piece of wire through the end of the knit tube to give you something to grasp with your pliers **(r)**.

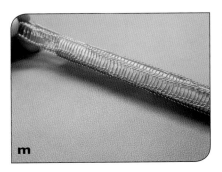

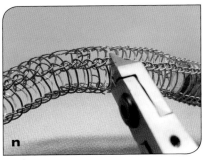

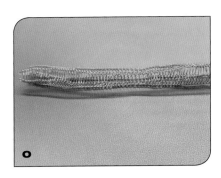

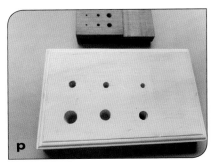

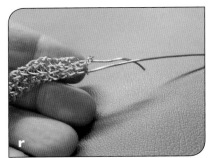

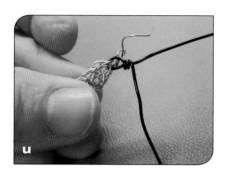

**18** Continue pulling the knit tube through progressively smaller holes until you get the desired thickness.

**19** Twist one end of the knit tube to close **(s)**.

**Making wire cones**

**20** Cut a 12" piece of 18-gauge wire in a coordinating color to make your cone end. Thread the end of the wire ¼" from the end of the knit tube. Bend the wire in half about 2" from the end **(t)**.

**21** Make a wrapped loop (Techniques, p. 11) **(u)**.

**22** Holding the wire by the loop, continue to wrap downward, gradually making the loops larger to create a cone over the end of the wrap **(v, w)**.

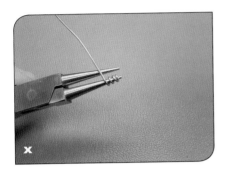

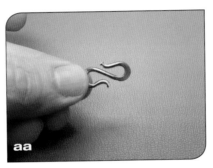

**23** Cut a 2" piece of 24-gauge wire. Make a loose coil at one end using your roundnose pliers **(x)**.

**24** String a round bead, a cube crystal, a rondelle, and a round bead on the wire, then thread the wire through the Viking knit segment, starting close to the coiled cap **(y)**.

**25** String a round bead on the wire and use roundnose pliers to loosely coil the wire down to the bead **(z)**.

**26** Continue this process, until you have filled the bracelet the way you like.

**27** Cut a 3" piece of 12-gauge wire and make an S-hook clasp (Techniques, p. 12) **(aa)**.

**28** Attach the S-hook to the cones at either end of the bracelet **(bb)**.

# New Beginnings
## earrings

**Techniques**
• • • • • • • • •
making Viking knit

making wrapped loops

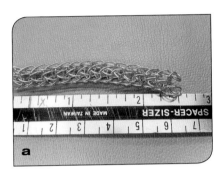

a

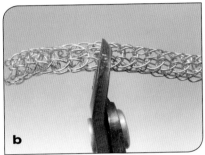

b

c

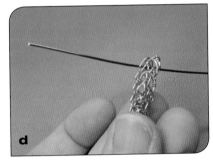

d

## Materials

- 18-gauge colored wire
- 24-gauge colored wire
- **2** 8mm rondelles
- **2** 3mm cube crystals
- **2** 3mm round beads
- **2** earring wires (optional)

## Tools

- Basic Tool Kit
- ½" wooden dowel
- Credit card
- Draw plate
- Painter's tape

## Instructions

**1** Follow instrauctions on pages 85–88 to create 2" of Viking knit using 24-gauge wire. Draw it down to 2½" **(a)**.

**2** Using flush wire cutters, cut the knit tube into two 1¼" sections **(b)**.

**3** Pinch both ends of each sections together by rolling the ends between your forefinger and thumb **(c)**.

**4** Cut a 4" piece of 18-gauge wire and thread 1" of the wire through the top of the knitted section **(d)**.

### TIP

This pair of earrings can be made with 2" of Viking knit used in the New Beginnings bracelet (p. 84).

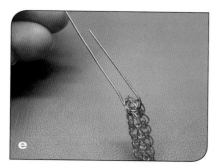

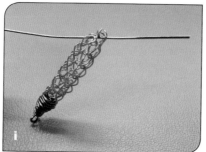

**5** Bend both ends of the wire parallel with the knit **(e)**.

**6** Wrap the short end of the wire around the longer wire loop **(f)**.

**7** Position roundnose pliers above the wrap and make a plain loop (Techniques, p. 10) **(g)**.

**8** Wrap the remaining length of wire down over the coil and over the first ¼" of the knit tube, creating a wire cone on the end of the knit tube **(h)**.

**9** Cut another 4" of 18-gauge wire and thread 1" of the wire through the bottom of the knit tube **(i)**.

**10** Wrap the short end of the wire around the longer wire loop **(j)**.

**11** String beads onto the wire. Use roundnose pliers to make a coil **(k)**.

**12** Use flush wire cutters to trim excess wire **(l)**.

**13** Make your own earring wires (Techniques, p. 15) or attach puchased earring wires **(m)**.

**14** Make a second earring to match the first.

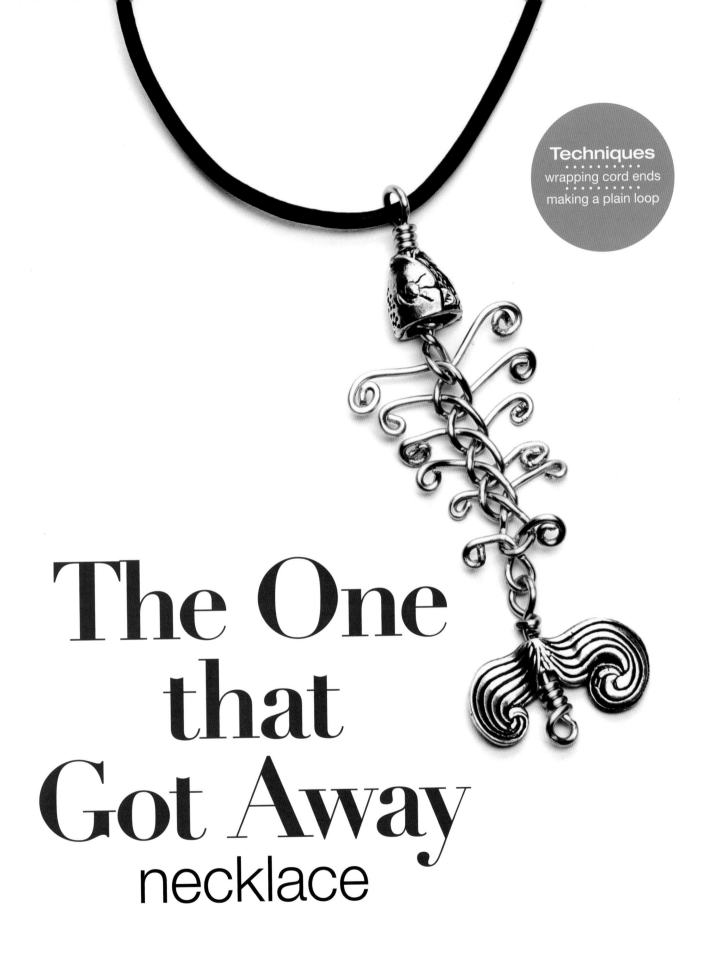

Techniques
· · · · · · · · · ·
wrapping cord ends
· · · · · · · · · ·
making a plain loop

# The One that Got Away
## necklace

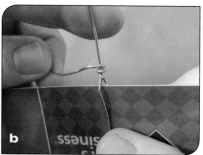
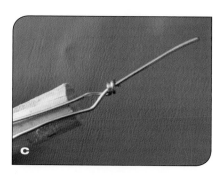
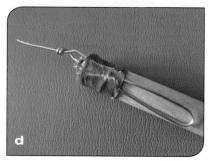
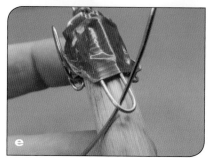
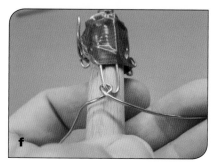

## Materials

- 16-gauge copper wire
- 18-gauge colored wire
- Silver-plated fish head and tail or make by hand from the pattern. (You might use resin, shrink plastic, polymer clay, ceramic, paper, metal, or enamel).
- 2mm leather cord

## Tools

- Basic Tool Kit
- ½" wooden dowel
- Anvil or bench block
- Credit card
- Domed chasing hammer
- Tape

## Instructions

**1** Working off an 18-gauge spool of wire, make one loop around the credit card, leaving a 2" tail **(a)**.

**2** Wrap the end of the wire around the top of the loop to close the loop **(b)**. Trim the excess wire.

**3** Slide the loop off of the card.

**4** Position the loop of wire at the top of the ½" dowel as shown **(c).**

**5** Using the tape, secure the wire to the dowel **(d)**. (Or you can do like I did and use the loops from "New Beginnings bracelet", p. 84 and tape up all but one loop.)

**6** Thread the end of the wire through the loop from the back **(e)**.

**7** Hold the loop end and cross the spool end of the wire over the short end of wire, creating a cursive "e" **(f)**. Wrap the wire around the dowel.

**fish head and tail pattern**

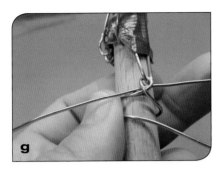

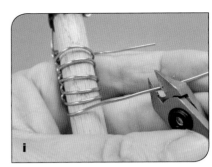

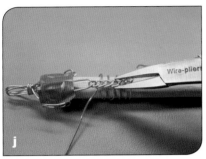

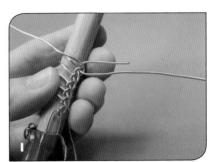

**8** Begin to make the "vertebrae" by pushing your wire from the right side in behind the "x" made by the first loop. Pull the wire, creating a loop similar to the one above and hold it with the thumb of your non-dominant hand to secure the size **(g)**. (Make sure your loops are the same size.)

**9** Repeat steps 7 and 8 to make as many "vertebrae" for your fish as you want. I made six **(h)**.

**10** When you have made all of the ribs, cut your working wire 2" long **(i)**.

**11** Pinch the loops with chainnose pliers **(j)**.

**12** Using a domed chasing hammer, gently tap down the loops **(k)**.

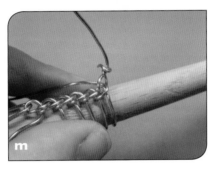

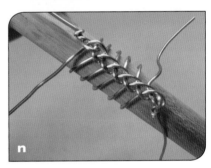

**13** Still working on the dowel, thread a 3" piece of 18-gauge wire up through the last loop and bend it up parallel to itself **(l)**.

**14** Make a one-turn loop using the short end of the wire. Cut off the excess wire.

**15** Thread a piece of 18-gauge wire through the loop at the bottom of the weave **(m)**. Cut the working loop off of the woven wires.

**16** Wrap this loop just like you did the wrap at the opposite end of the weave.

**17** Remove the ribs from the ½" dowel **(n)**.

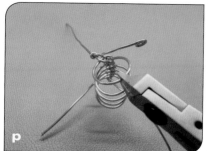

**18** Spiral the end of the 1" remainder of wire **(o)**.

**19** Cut the first coil in half **(p)**.

**20** Allow a ¼" of wire for the spirals at the ends of each rib. Use roundnose pliers to make each tiny spiral.

**21** Cut the next rib from the back of the coil and repeat.

**22** Continue this process, getting gradually shorter as you go. Tweak your rib lengths and coils to make sure they look right.

**23** Place the fish "ribs" on an anvil or bench block and gently tap them down **(q)**.

**24** Thread the head of the fish on the end of the longest bones. Make a wrapped loop to secure it in place (Techniques, p. 10) **(r)**.

**25** Repeat the previous step for the tail of the fish **(s)**.

**26** Hang the fish on a 2mm leather cord. Wrap the ends of the cord (Techniques, p. 11) **(t)**.

**27**. Make a clasp or add a purchased one.

# Sea Foam Web
## necklace

**Techniques**
· · · · · · · · ·
making a shepherd's hook clasp
· · · · · · · · ·
making jump rings

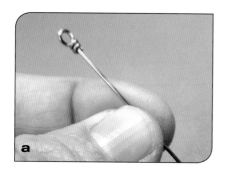

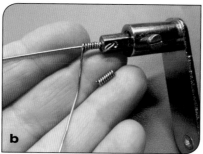

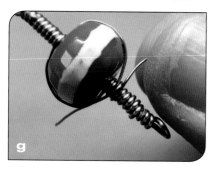

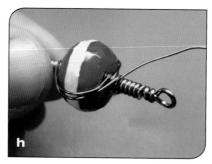

**5** Make a wrapped loop above the coil **(d)**.

**6** Working from the spool of 26-gauge wire, make one tight wrap around the wire as close to the opening of the bead as you can get **(e)**.

**7** Wrap over the bead on one side and loop the wire tightly around the coil as close to the bead as possible **(f)**.

**8** Wrap the wire over the bead on the opposite side and coil around the wire, one coil from the first wrap **(g)**.

**9** Repeat step 7, but move over one coil. Make sure the section of wire going around the bead is tucked neatly under the previous wire **(h)**.

## Materials

- 18-gauge colored wire
- 20-gauge colored wire
- 26-gauge colored wire
- 9 8mm faceted crystal rondelles
- 8 14mm rondelle glass beads

## Tools

- Basic Tool Kit
- Mister Twister wire coiler or 1mm wooden dowel

## Instructions

**1** Cut a 3" piece of 20-gauge wire for each 14mm rondelle bead.

**2** Make a wrapped loop at one end of each wire (Techniques, p. 11) **(a)**.

**3** Using a Mister Twister (or wooden dowel) make two eight-rotation coils from 20-gauge wire for each 14mm rondelle **(b)**.

**4** String a coil, a 14mm rondelle, and a coil **(c)**.

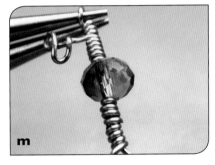

**10** Continue steps 7 and 8 until you get to the end of the wire **(i, j)**.

**11** Using flush wire cutters, trim the wire flush with the coil and the starter length **(k)**.

**12** Repeat steps 4–11 for all of the 14mm rondelles **(l)**.

**13** Using your Mister Twister (or wooden dowel), cut a 2" piece of 20-gauge wire for each 8mm rondelle. Make a wrapped loop at one end of each wire.

**14** Make two, four-rotation coils for each 8mm rondelle.

**15** String a coil, an 8mm rondelle, and a coil onto a wire. Make a plain loop at the end of each wire to secure the beads (Techniques, p. 10) **(m)**.

**16** Make a 4mm jump ring for each set of beads using a Mister Twister (or a wooden dowel) (Techniques, p. 12) **(n)**.

**TIP**
**Make sure to flush cut all of your jump rings (o).**

**17** Using flatnose and chainnose pliers, attach the bead components with jump rings **(p)**.

**18** Make a closed shepherd's hook clasp from 18-gauge wire and attach it to the jump ring of the end crystal component.

**19** Attach a jump ring at the opposite end of the necklace.

# Sea Foam Web
## earrings

**Techniques**
· · · · · · · · · ·
making wrapped
loops
· · · · · · · · · ·
making earring
wires

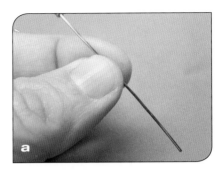

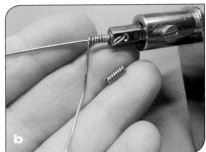

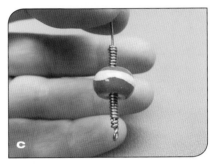

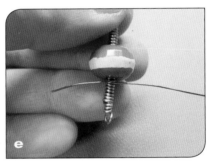

## Materials

- 20-gauge colored wire
- 26-gauge colored wire
- 2 14mm rondelles
- 2 8mm faceted crystal rondelles
- 2 earring wires (optional)

## Tools

- Basic Tool Kit
- Mister Twister wire coiler or 1mm wooden dowel

## Instructions

**1** Cut a 3" piece of 20-gauge wire for each 14mm rondelle.

**2** Make a plain loop at one end of each wire (Techniques, p. 10) **(a)**.

**3** Using a Mister Twister (or wooden dowel), make two eight-rotation coils from 20-gauge wire for each 14mm rondelle **(b)**.

**4** String a coil, a 14mm rondelle, and a coil **(c)**.

**5** Make a plain loop at the open end of the wire to secure the beads **(d)**.

**6** Working from the spool of 26-gauge wire, make a tight wrap around the wire as close to the opening of the bead as you can get **(e)**.

**7** Wrap the wire over the bead on one side and loop the wire tightly around the coil as close to the bead as possible **(f)**.

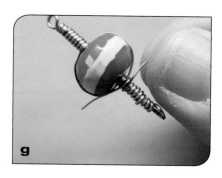

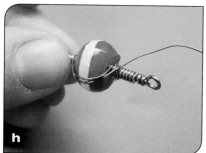

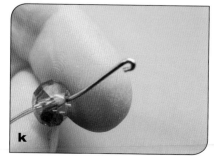

**8** Wrap the wire over the bead on the opposite side and coil the wire one coil above the first wrap **(g)**.

**9** Repeat steps 7 and 8, but move over one coil. Make sure the wire going around the bead is tucked neatly under the previous wire **(h)**.

**10** Repeat steps 8 and 9 until you reach the end of the wire **(i)**.

**11** Using flush wire cutters, trim the wire flush with the coil and trim off the starter length **(j)**.

**12** Cut a 3" piece of 24-gauge wire and make a tight pinch at one end with chainnose pliers. String an 8mm rondelle **(k)**.

**13** Make a plain loop and attach the crystal rondelle to the end of the wrapped bead **(l)**.

**14** Repeat steps 4–13 to make the second earring.

**15** Make your own earring wires (Techniques, p. 15) or attach purchased earring wires to each dangle **(m)**.

# Dragon Scales
## bracelet

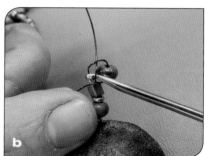

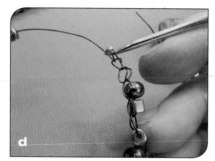

## Materials

- 18-gauge colored wire
- 26-gauge colored wire
- **110** assorted
  3mm–4mm beads

## Tools

- Basic Tool Kit
- Crochet needle, size B/1
  (2.25mm)

## Instructions

**1** Pre-string all of the beads (in a random pattern) directly onto your spool of 26-gauge wire **(a)**.

**2** Make a loop in the wire next to the last bead. Insert the crochet hook and make the first link of a chain stitch (Techniques, p. 10) **(b)**.

**3** Continue with the chain, incorporating a bead in each link, until you have a 4½" segment **(c)**.

**4** Make two stitches in your chain without beads **(d)**. Pull up a bead and continue for 4½" more.

**5** Repeat steps 2 and 3 two more times so you have four segments.

**6** Cut a 6" piece of 18-gauge wire. Loop the wire through the section of the un-beaded links of chain **(e)**.

**7** Wrap the tail around the wire stem, making a wrapped loop (Techniques, p. 11) **(f)**.

**8** String a few beads on the wire **(g)**.

**9** Fold the remaining wire in half **(h)**.

**10** Make a set of wraps with the tail of the wire **(i)**.

**11** Make a tight pinch at the folded end of the wires **(j)**.

**12** Shape the remaining wire into a hook **(k)**.

**13** Pull the loose ends of the wires together on the opposite end of the bracelet and string a few beads over them.

**14** Cut about 18" of 18-gauge wire off of your coil.

**15** Use roundnose pliers and make a loop in the center of the wire.

**16** Thread the remaining 26-gauge wire through the loop **(l)**.

**17** Wrap it around the loop, securing the crochet beads to the loop made in 18-gauge wire.

**18** Make a toggle ring and attach it to the end of the bracelet (Techniques, p. 14) **(m)**.

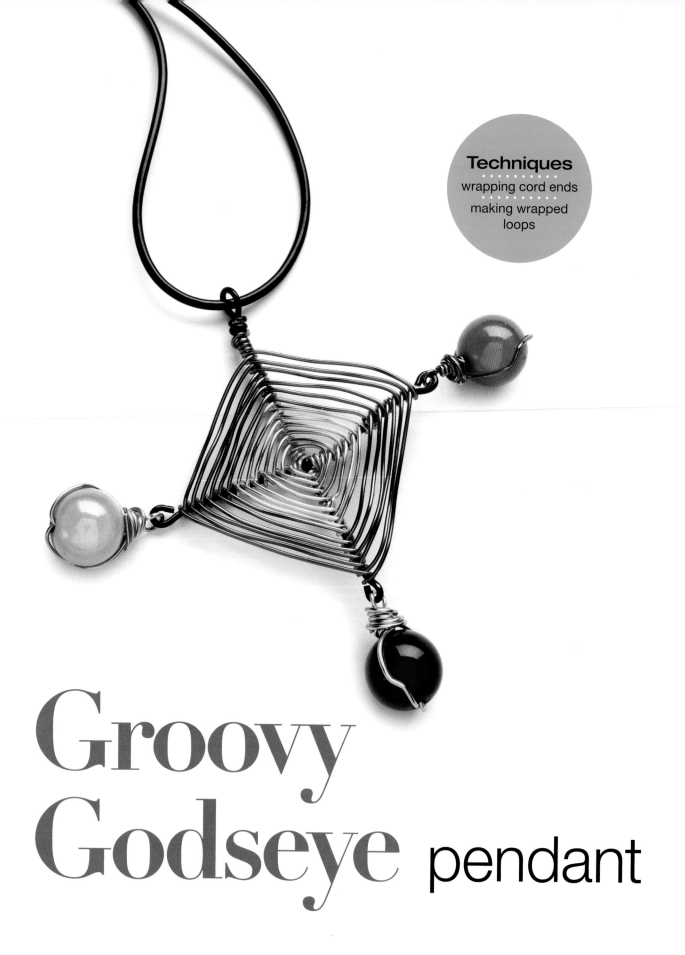

# Groovy Godseye pendant

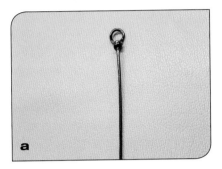

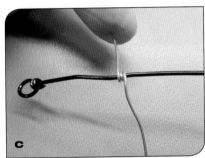

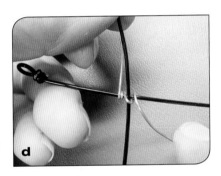

## Instructions

**1** Cut a 6" piece of 18-gauge wire and make a wrapped loop at one end (Techniques, p. 11) **(a)**.

**2** Measure the unwrapped length of wire in step 1 and cut a piece of 18-gauge wire that same length **(b)**.

**3** Using one color of 20-gauge wires, wrap two loops in the center of the 18-gauge wire **(c)**.

**4** Position the second piece of 18-gauge wire directly next to the loops. Pull the 20-gauge wire up and over the 18-gauge wire, securing it with two more loops on the other side **(d)**.

## Materials

- 18-gauge aluminum wire
- 20-gauge wire in four different colors
- Leather cord
- **3** 12mm accent beads

## Tools

- Basic Tool Kit

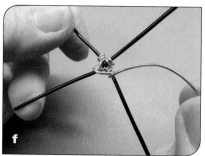

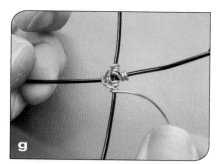

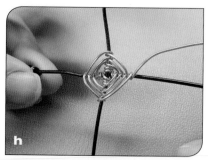

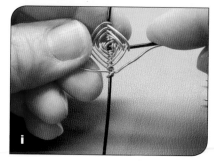

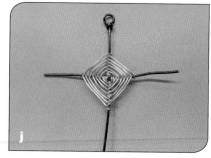

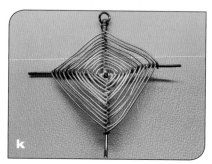

**5** Move the 20-gauge wire over to the next 18-gauge wire and wrap two loops.

**6** Move to the fourth wire from behind and wrap two loops **(e)**.

**7** Wrap from the last coil across the wire loop one time and then around the next wire **(f)**.

**8** Wrap your wire over the next wire to the right and make one loop **(g)**.

**9** Continue around the wires in this manner for three weaves **(h)**.

**10** Choose a second color and wrap it around one loop **(i)**.

**11** Wrap this wire around until you have three weaves **(j)**.

**12** Add two more colors of wire, weaving each one three times around the base wires **(k)**.

**13** Use roundnose pliers to make a plain loop at the end of each base wire (Techniques, p 10) **(l)**.

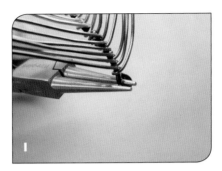

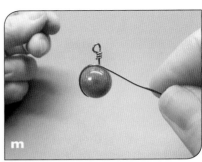

**14** Cut a 4" piece of 20-gauge wire and make a wrapped loop on one end. String an accent bead onto the wire and bend the wire up and over the bead **(m)**.

**15** Coil the end of the wire around the top of the bead **(n)**.

**16** Bring the wire back down to the bottom of the bead and thread it back through the hole of the bead **(o)**.

**17** Wrap the remaining wire lazily around the original coil **(p)**. Repeat steps 14–17 with the two remaining beads.

**18** Open the loops made at the ends of the wires and attach the beads **(q)**.

**19** String the pendant on a leather cord. Wrap each end of the leather (Techniques, p. 11) and add a clasp made from 18-gauge wire.

# Acknowledgments

I would first like to thank my loving husband Norm and my sweet son Chase for putting up with me while writing this book. Life can be less than normal when I'm in the book-writing mode. Thanks to my daughter Nora and my granddaughter Ever for understanding the limited time I had to be with them while I was working on this book.

I want to give a very special thank you to Karin Van Voorhees for asking me to write this book and a grateful thank you to Parawire and WireJewelry.com for providing me with all the beautiful colored wire used in the projects.

There were some components used in several of the projects made by artist friends of mine, and I'd like to thank them for allowing me to create jewelry using their art. Thank you to Chase Allendale for the boro cabochon used in the Portal Pendant; to Barbara McGuire for the polymer clay beads used in the Chrysalis earrings; to Julie McIntyre for the lampwork beads used in the Bold & Bitters earrings; to Michele McCarthy for the beads used in the Blue Fish bracelet and earrings; and to Niki Thornburg for the lampwork beads used in the Sacré Bleu earrings.

There were several artists who donated pieces of their art for projects that did not make it into this particular book—but fear not my beautiful friends, you will see your pieces combined with my efforts in the near future.

Thank you to my editor Dianne Wheeler and her staff for being patient with me this year. My teaching schedule was hectic to say the least, and the creation of this book was forced into every spare moment available–before, between, during, and after classes.

I love and appreciate all you do for me Norm, Chase, Nora, Ever, Mom, Dad, Trey, Olen, JJ, Donny, Bobby, Louise, Kim, Steve, Dari, Chuck, Margaret, the Apache Girls, all of my students, fellow instructors, show promoters, and friends. Thank You.

# About the Author

*Kim St. Jean* graduated from the University of South Carolina Aiken with a BA in Education. She taught in the public schools of South Carolina and North Carolina for 10 years. In 1998, she finally decided to follow her dream of entrepreneurship. She opened her first brick and mortar business in Belmont, NC.

Soon after, her husband Norm left his career in textiles and joined her. They quickly outgrew the little boutique and moved to the Charlotte Merchandise Mart, becoming a large wholesaler and trade supplier of beads and findings. Among those beads were Swarovski crystals.

Along the way, a representative from Swarovski, Kim Paquette, met with Kim and asked her to go to Tucson, AZ to teach for them. This was the beginning of a life changing career for both Kim and Norm. Since that first national teaching opportunity, Kim has become an award winning instructor, designer, and author.

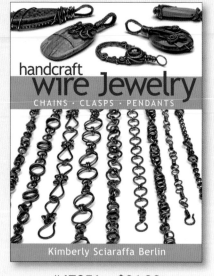
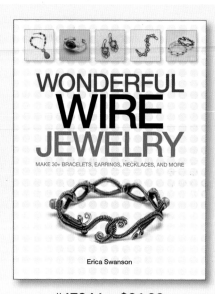
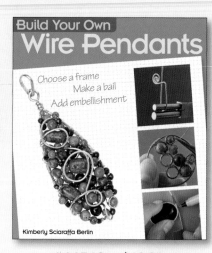